WHAT WE
OWE IRAQ

Noah Feldman

WHAT WE OWE IRAQ

War and the Ethics of Nation Building

PRINCETON UNIVERSITY PRESS
PRINCETON AND OXFORD

Copyright © 2004 by Princeton University Press
Published by Princeton University Press, 41 William Street,
Princeton, New Jersey 08540
In the United Kingdom: Princeton University Press,
3 Market Place, Woodstock,
Oxfordshire OX20 1SY

Library of Congress Cataloging-in-Publication Data

Feldman, Noah, 1970–
What we owe Iraq : war and the ethics of
nation building / Noah Feldman.
  p. cm.
Includes bibliographical references and index.
ISBN: 0-691-12179-6 (acid-free paper)
1. Postwar reconstruction—Iraq. 2. Iraq War, 2003—Peace.
3. Newly independent states—Case studies. I. Title.
    DS79.769.F45   2004
  956.7044′31—dc22   2004016041

British Library Cataloging-in-Publication Data is available

This book has been composed in Dante

Printed on acid-free paper. ∞

pup.princeton.edu

Printed in the United States of America

1   3   5   7   9   10   8   6   4   2

To the memory of
Robert Nozick

CONTENTS

WHAT WE
OWE IRAQ

Introduction

LATE ONE NIGHT IN MAY 2003, I WAS IN A MILITARY transport plane somewhere over the Mediterranean, on my way to a stint as constitutional adviser to the American occupation authorities in Iraq. In the dozen or so rows of seats that had been jerry-rigged in the open belly of the aircraft, most of the passengers—all in various aspects of the advising business—were dozing, shivering slightly for the last time before we hit the Baghdad heat. The adrenaline pumping through me, I was rereading the best modern book on the Iraqi Shiʿaʾ[1] and hastily trying to teach myself some Iraqi colloquial dialect.

Pausing to take in the moment, I glanced around at my new colleagues. Those who were awake were reading intently. When I saw what they were reading, though, a chill crept over me, too. Not one seemed to need a refresher on Iraq or the Gulf region. Without exception, they were reading new books on the American occupation and reconstruction of Germany and Japan.

My initial shock at my colleagues' reading matter was almost purely situational. Although it is possible to draw some more than superficial analogies between Baʿthism and National Socialism,[2] Iraq was nothing like postwar Germany and Japan. Economic, political, social, and cultural conditions in Iraq after the U.S. invasion were distinct from any occupation situation that anyone had ever encountered, and if there was to be any hope of handling the situation effectively, the first step was surely to immerse oneself in what information was available about the country. The task felt classically orientalist, in the sense of gathering knowledge in order to exert control; but what other choice was there? Once you had agreed to go to Iraq as part of the occupation, you could go ignorant, or you could try to learn as much as possible.

But there was another, deeper problem with thinking of Iraq in terms borrowed from the nation-building experiences of the post–World War II era. We were occupying Iraq for reasons very different from those underlying our occupations of Germany and Japan. The most obvious difference was that the Axis powers had attacked us, and that we had then, with no other choice, fought and defeated them in a world war of unprecedented horror. By contrast, our war in Iraq, framed though it might have been in terms of preemptive self-protection, had been essentially voluntary. More to the point, however, the *purposes* of our occupation and reconstruction efforts in the second half of the 1940s were fundamentally different from the purposes of the task we were poised to undertake in Iraq. Different strategic objectives call for different tactics; but that is not all. The different purposes of contemporary nation building also call for a new and different ethical approach, one grounded in a normative evaluation of what we set out to achieve, the means and attitudes we adopt in the process, and a realistic sense of what success or failure would look like. We need, in short, an ethics of nation building suitable to our circumstances.

The place to begin the enquiry after such an ethics is with a clear-eyed, honest assessment of the purposes of nation building today, whether in Iraq or elsewhere—and that is the topic of the first chapter, in which I offer an explanation of how nation building can serve the nation builder's security interests, and how failed or incomplete nation building can harm them. In brief, I argue that strong countries like the United States and the Western European powers have an interest in building nation-states that seem reasonably legitimate to their citizens, because failed states and those perceived as illegitimately imposed from outside are likely to generate terror. I then defend self-protective nation building from the ethical challenge that its motives doom it to immorality.

The second chapter confronts the legacy of paternalism that, inherited from the ideology of empire, pervades the theory and practice of nation building today. I propose that nation building can be salvaged ethically only if it is stripped down to the modest proposition that the nation builder exercises temporary political authority as trustee on behalf of the people being governed, in much the same way that an elected government does. The fact that nation builders do not stand for election means they must authorize alternative means for the people whom they are governing to monitor their performance: free speech, assembly, and the active participation in government of the citizens of the country being ruled from the outside.

In the third and final chapter I consider how elections ought to figure in the nation-building process. Too much has been made of the capacity of elections to reflect the general will, and too little of their value in revealing voters' leadership preferences and in checking the arbitrary exercise of power. I propose that elections must be understood as the midpoint of the nation-building undertaking, not the end of the nation builder's obligations toward the country in question. In particular, I argue that the nation builder must not compromise its duty to provide security so as to facilitate political negotiation among the people who must shape the future for themselves—despite the likelihood that the nation builder will be sorely tempted to cut and run.

In each chapter, I draw examples from the U.S.-led occupation of Iraq in 2003–4, a distinctive moment that poses the ethical dilemmas of nation building more starkly than do the post–Cold War nation-building projects undertaken by UN-authorized transitional administrations in Somalia, Bosnia, Kosovo, East Timor, and Afghanistan. From May 2003, when it was formally organized to replace the short-lived Office of Reconstruction and Humanitarian Assistance, the Coalition Provisional Authority (CPA) operated for more than a year in Iraq as an occupation government before transforming itself on June 28, 2004, into a U.S. embassy with extraordinary advisory capacities. During this period, the civilian administrator, L. Paul Bremer III, reported to the president of the United States through the secretary of defense. Although the United Kingdom participated in the CPA, sending a series of special representatives who in principle ranked alongside Bremer, and although other Coalition participants like Australia and Italy took roles in the CPA as well, the CPA functioned largely as an American show with British input.

In the context of UN-approved nation building, serious problems of conflict of interest, paternalism, and self-determination are sometimes shrugged off with a gesture toward the authorization of "the international community." By contrast, the case of U.S.-led nation building in Iraq precludes easy answers—and continues to do so even after formal political authority has shifted to Iraqis, with the recognition of the Security Council. Coalition troops remain on the ground in large numbers, and others will likely stay on for years. Nation building in Iraq is far from over. Our responsibilities to Iraq, and to ourselves, are not yet discharged. The ethical problems that this book considers will therefore remain alive in Iraq for years to come; and they will recur, in identifiable forms, whenever nation building is contemplated or undertaken.

A further distinctive feature of nation building in Iraq is, of course, the way the old regime ceased to be: not by internal collapse, but by overwhelming military force from without. Throughout its brief and eventful life, the CPA's status reflected legal ambiguity about the invasion of Iraq—which the Coalition depicted as authorized by a UN Security Council resolution, but which was never subsequently ratified by the Security Council, only acknowledged.[3] In this book, I do not propose to consider the legality or wisdom of the U.S.-led removal of the regime of Saddam Hussein. Nor shall I even pose the related, extraordinarily complex question of when international intervention is justified, if ever. Other and better minds than mine have devoted enormous energy to the subject without exhausting it—and the debate, albeit altered by September 11, is still on.[4] I want to focus, rather, on what happens after intervention is an accomplished fact—when the old regime is gone and a foreign power is calling the shots, whether it be the United Nations, NATO, or, as in 2003–4 in Iraq, a far narrower, U.S.-led coalition. On the ethical aspects of this topic there has been relatively little systematic thinking in the post–Cold War environment.[5] We have a crop of memoirs about war and reconstruction in the former Yugoslavia,[6] and some excellent studies of transitional justice and war-crimes tribunals.[7] There is also a growing literature on the how-to side of nation building.[8] Inspired by the problem of failed states, a small literature has grown up revisiting the option of international trusteeship.[9] We do not yet have, however, a satisfactory account of why we should want to do such a thing as build nations and what the relevant principles are for making ethical sense of this goal.

The aim of this book is to jump-start an urgent conversation about the ethics of nation building. In the midst of all the heated, high-priority arguments about what policy would best serve U.S. interests in Iraq, it sometimes seems as though no one is asking what obligations we might have to the Iraqis whose government we deposed and whose country we occupied. The need is all the more pressing because of the tremendous complexities of the developing situation in Iraq, but it will persist even after Iraq recedes from the headlines. Realism and protective self-interest will play crucial parts in this conversation, to be sure; in what follows I seek to analyze problems of violence, security, and nation building in terms of the strategic incentives of various participants in a complex, multitiered engagement, because I do not think an account without this perspective would be very useful in the real world. But this is not the whole story, either. If ethics are to be taken seriously, we must also consider our problem from the standpoints of law, democratic theory, and moral principle.

In the hope of rendering the discussion concrete, I have included plenty of particulars of the situation on the ground in Iraq, including circumstances I encountered personally. In doing so, I want to provide a taste of how ethical problems and doubts present themselves in the real time of nation building.[10] But I also aim to do something more, something that a few astute listeners noticed (and to which some strongly objected) when I delivered an earlier version of my argument as the Walter E. Edge Lectures at Princeton in April 2004. I want to implicate you, the reader, in the subjective "we" of ethical obligation, no matter your views on war and reconstruction in Iraq or elsewhere. If you are reading this, I want to suggest, you can be called to account for your own role in considering and debating the ethics of nation building, and in shaping collective decisions for the future. This claim may be controversial, but making it seems to me the only point of an argument in ethics.[11] After all, there is no coercive authority in a book. All I can do is suggest a point of view, give my reasons for holding it, and invite you to try it on for size. What you do next is up to you.

CHAPTER ONE

Nation Building: Objectives

TO BEGIN, THEN, LET ME PROPOSE AN ACCOUNT OF WHY the United States has engaged in nation building in Iraq, and how this undertaking differs from earlier American nation-building efforts. From the outset of the Cold War, the American objective in nation building was to create rich, stable, independent, capital-driven states in order to strengthen the American alliance that was then called "the free world" against the Soviet Union and *its* satellites. This approach met with some remarkable successes—South Korea's rags-to-riches story springs to mind—but its paradigmatic successful cases were Germany and Japan themselves. Nation building in Germany and Japan aimed to transform powerful enemies into prosperous allies in an emerging new struggle with the Soviet Union. Knowing that these nations had the capacity for unity, organization, and productivity, we sought to make them over to move them into our column. With U.S. supervision and assistance, America's former enemies were made into its economic competitors for no better reason than that a strong Germany and a strong Japan could help the United States survive—or, as it turned out, win—the Cold War. The objective was not to build democratic states for the benefit of their citizens—a glance at U.S. support of authoritarian regimes from Southeast Asia to Latin America suffices to prove that. It was far less important that Germany and Japan be democratic than that they be capitalist and rich. The objective was to create nations that would, by a complex combination of external pressure and the financial self-interest of elites, take our side in a global war and be useful to us in it.[1]

Today, with the Cold War behind us, the objective in nation building cannot be to gain allies in some global war against an easily identifiable enemy. At once more modest and more ambitious, our objective must be to build stable, legitimate states whose own citizens will not seek to destroy us. States that enjoy legitimacy among the overwhelming majority of their own citizens and that allow the possibility of changing policy by democratic means serve our common interest in collective security. The best route to self-preservation lies in the creation of states that respect individual liberties, both political and civil. In short: the objective of nation building ought to be the creation of reasonably legitimate, reasonably liberal democracies.

The threat that powerful nations face today is not total destruction by ballistic missiles. It is massive, but nonetheless not total, destruction by the means we are accustomed to call "terrorist." The danger posed by terrorism is arguably not existential in the same sense as the Cold War threat: attacks like those of September 11 may or may not have the capacity to destroy us utterly. A smuggled nuclear weapon could destroy lower Manhattan, while the Soviets had the capacity to destroy every population center in the country. Yet there can be no question that terrorism is today the greatest threat to the United States, to its allies, and even to its erstwhile enemies like the states of the former Soviet Union.

Few words are thrown around more loosely than "terrorism," so let me offer a functional definition. Most contemporary uses of the word "terrorism" are trying to describe a type of violence perpetrated by nonstate actors against civilian targets. This definition is not uncontroversial, and there are many who would immediately point out that it unfairly excludes state terrorism, executed by state actors against civilians. But let me simply point out that the need for the adjective "state" in the phrase "state terrorism" strongly suggests, as a descriptive matter, that our ordinary English-language usage of the term "terrorism" encompasses only nonstate violence. The reason I suggest that the greatest threat today comes from terrorism is not simply that the attacks of September 11 still loom large in all our minds. When speaking of terrorism, one lapses easily into the error of overgeneralizing from recent, salient experience— falling prey to what behavioral psychologists and economists call the "availability heuristic"—and I am trying hard to avoid this mistake.[2] Rather, the reason to consider terrorism the gravest present threat to us, above the missiles of hostile powers like North Korea, and above even the epochal growth (and potential belligerence) of China, is that state actors for the last half century—and indeed beyond—have shown a consistent propensity to respond to the negative reinforcement of threatened destruction. Leaders of states almost never attack other states or peoples if they know to a relatively high probability that doing so will result in their removal or death. One could call this a rational-actor model of the state, but introducing the subtle topic of rationality here may actually obfuscate more than it clarifies. It will be enough to say that North Korea, for all its weapons capability, has not attacked South Korea and almost certainly will not attack so long as its leaders understand that such an attack would result in their deaths. (The same could arguably be said of the nuclear face-off between Pakistan and India, which resembles the Cold War writ small in its promise of mutually assured destruction.) Because no state could directly attack the United States without guaranteeing the death and destruction of its leaders, we can be reasonably certain of being safe from such an attack. Some states could conceivably try to inflict violence without being blamed for it by supporting third-party terrorists, as Libya did during the 1980s and early 1990s. But, as demonstrated by the eventual response of Muammar Qadhafi to U.S. bombings and broader economic sanctions, such indirect violence can usually be traced to its source and deterred.[3] Because it is difficult for states to avoid responsibility for their actions, deterrence is on the whole a reliable method for dealing with state-based threats.

Nonstate violent actors, on the other hand, typically do not respond to the threat of their own destruction in the predictable way that state actors do. They are prepared to attack even when the consequences for themselves will be dire. One reason may be that nonstate actors are prepared to die for their causes, whereas ordinary government officials are less likely to lay down their lives; but states also spawn warriors ready to give their lives for heroism, nationalism, or faith, so this is unlikely to be the major reason why terrorists do not respond predictably to retaliatory threat. More likely, the reason terrorists cannot reliably be deterred as states can is that retaliation against terror is often very nonspecific. Unlike states, terrorist organizations can melt away. Al-Qaʿida used the Taliban state in Afghanistan as its staging ground; and after the U.S. invasion, that state ceased to exist while al-Qaʿida has maintained its shadowy presence almost to the degree that it did before. Government leaders may try to disappear, as Saddam did, but experience suggests that it is harder for them to avoid capture than it is for terrorists. Mullah Omar of the Taliban remains at large, but he was always more of a rebel leader than a head of state, preserving his anonymity by never appearing in public unmasked.

The point sounds obvious, but it bears repeating, because too often the behavior of terrorists is thought to be distinctive solely because of their extreme ideology. Unlike states, terrorist organizations cannot be found in any one particular spot. You cannot eliminate them by occupying the radio station and the national bank. This is an important reason why terrorist leaders generally seem more confident than state leaders that other hydra heads will replace them should theirs be cut off. It is not that terrorists are necessarily any more certain of the justice of their causes than are the leaders of governments. It is just that when the apparatus of the state has been captured, no new "president" can emerge without the consent of the occupier—all that is possible is an insurgency. Kill Osama bin Laden, however, and all it takes for another to assume his role is to tell the organization's adherents and supporters that he has taken charge. Indeed, it would even be possible to kill *every* present al-Qaᶜida member and for the organization to be reborn in the next moment via a new group of persons who assumed the mission. Like the Dread Pirate Roberts in the movie, all the nonstate actor needs to perpetuate himself is a name.

Terrorism, then, tops our threat list because of its nonresponsiveness to the disincentives we have been accustomed to use. It follows that our predominant security goal ought to be reducing the risk of terrorist attack. That does not mean reducing the risk at any cost. There are those already who believe that the United States poses a greater risk to world security than do the terrorists themselves—a frightening thought, although one that for the most part still seems to be meant rhetorically. We cannot defensibly take every step that would reduce the terrorist threat to zero, any more than we could justify putting the country in lockdown to prevent any crime. But we can, we may, and we ought to take steps to reduce the threat of terrorism to the extent we can do so in a way that is consistent with our moral commitments. Specifically, we can identify the reduction of the threat of terror as a permissible objective—and indeed the primary objective—for our nation-building efforts.

Let me hasten to distinguish two different possible versions of the argument that reducing the threat of nonstate violence against civilians ought to be the aim of nation building. One possible approach—let's call it the "war on terror"—aims to create and nurture stable states so that they can crush the nonstate terrorists who threaten their existence and our lives. This view begins with the plausible claim that weak or failing states are breeding grounds for nonstate violence. Terrorists in weak states may aim to assume control of the state in which they live—nonstate Serbian militias in

Bosnia, for example—or their long-term objective may be to gain control of some other neighboring states, as in the case of Sierra Leonean rebels hunkered down in Liberia. Still another possibility is that the terrorists are opportunistically gaining a foothold in the weak state to launch attacks on distant enemies—more or less al-Qaʿida's posture in Taliban Afghanistan.

From the premise that weak states breed terror, the theorists of the war on terror reason that what we need are strong states with the capacity to suppress resistance. Rather than seeking to strengthen weak states by, for example, encouraging economic or political practices that might win the loyalties of a larger number of citizens, the "war on terror" approach focuses on consolidating states' coercive power. The government of Colombia must be strengthened with military aid so it can subdue the FARC; Peru must be powerful enough to shut down the Shining Path. Politics and wealth redistribution do not ordinarily figure as strengthening devices. We can be glad, maintain the advocates of the war on terror, that the Egyptian government under Hosni Mubarak proved itself durable enough during the 1990s to deal with the terrorists who sought its overthrow, and we must help strengthen the Pakistani state, supporting the vulnerable-looking Pervez Musharraf so that he does not fall to the radical Islamist terrorists who made some dozen attempts on his life in 2003–4 alone.

According to this view, we can comfortably say that we are at war with "terrorism" as a phenomenon because, with the Cold War over, our interests are always aligned with states against nonstate violent actors. Those states could be dangerous abroad and oppressive at home, but because their leaders are likely to respond to our external disincentive, they will be highly unlikely to attack us. States that self-consciously export terror are very unlikely to direct that terror against us, because doing so is just too risky. The ones we need to fear are the nonstate actors whom we cannot successfully discourage on our own. We will never know as much about how to defeat these terrorists as will their local governments; so we should back those governments in their local wars against terrorism to save ourselves. In a globalized environment, nowhere is more than a day's plane ride away. Under these conditions, terrorism anywhere is dangerous everywhere.

Notice that this realist account of the war on terror would not have supported the American-led invasion of Iraq. Whatever its considerable demerits under the genocidal Saddam, Iraq was a strong state. Although supporters of the Iraq war who also purported to care about the war on terror tried to assimilate the two by claiming that Saddam supported international terror, the evidence for this claim was slight, perhaps slighter even than the evidence for Saddam's weapons of mass destruction. Beyond the evidentiary problem, there was the further difficulty that Saddam had always shown himself to be motivated by a marked self-preservation instinct. (He had, after all, survived the invasion of Kuwait, gambling correctly that the United States would not want to take on the responsibility of governing Iraq that would have followed inexorably from a march on Baghdad.)

Invading Iraq in 2003, defeating and then disbanding the Iraqi army, created in Iraq a weak state—or maybe no state at all—in lieu of the strong one that had existed. The invasion and its aftermath thereby inaugurated a rich, new potential breeding environment for terror. The strength of the realist argument for the war on terror is one major reason why so many in the American foreign policy establishment opposed the war in Iraq after they had supported the war in Afghanistan, which in theory at least sought to replace a weak state that hosted terror with a stronger state that would not. It is also why post hoc critics of the Iraq war are not merely posturing when they assert that the war did not make the United States safer from the threat of terror. In fact, it could reasonably be argued that the occupation of Iraq not only created an environment in which terror could emerge, but gave Iraqis and other Muslims hostile to the American presence in the region an excellent excuse for new terror.

Notwithstanding the evident appeal of foreign-policy realism in a dangerous world, I believe that this version of the "war on terror" argument, with its generally applicable principle of supporting strong states against nonstate violence, is ultimately unsatisfying and misplaced. To begin with, such a war on terror is likely to be self-defeating. Where many citizens think the government is illegitimate, we are likely to find terrorist resistance continuing despite the exercise of increased force by the repressive state. This is not to deny that autocratic states can achieve local victories: Egypt really did break the backs of its local Islamist terrorist resistance over the course of the decade that followed Sadat's assassination.[4] Repression can, on occasion, defeat terror within a given country. In some cases, especially where the government in question enjoys a high degree of internal legitimacy, strengthening it to facilitate its fight against domestic terrorists may turn out to be a productive strategy. But at least some terrorist organizations will turn out to be highly mobile, so that displacing them will have unintended consequences. Beat them in one place, and they will look elsewhere for leverage. A cadre of Egyptian Islamist terrorists, defeated and thus displaced from their traditional battle against the Egyptian state in the 1990s, joined forces with Osama bin Laden to create al-Qaʿida.

The upshot is that not only weak or failed states unintentionally "breed" terrorism. Democratically illegitimate states do, too—especially when citizens perceive their regimes to have been imposed by outside forces that can themselves be targeted for terrorist attack.[5] Al-Qaʿida grew out of bin Laden's opposition to the Saudi state; the group made the United States a target less out of outrage at American moral corruption than because of U.S. support for Saudi Arabia, which bin Laden conceptualized as an illegitimate occupation of Muslim lands. In al-Qaʿida's perceptual scheme, the United States is the "far enemy," while the "near enemy" is not Israel but the Saudi monarchy itself. Palestinian terrorism has grown under conditions in the West Bank and Gaza in which the "government"—whether one considers that to be the Palestinian Authority, the Israeli occupational administration, both, or neither—appears to ordinary Palestinians illegitimate and externally imposed. In general, Islamist terrorists have long been motivated by their grievances against the authoritarian states in which they live.[6]

Of course there can be deeply divergent views about what constitutes a legitimate government. Timothy McVeigh, the Oklahoma City bomber, was influenced by a domestic movement that believed the U.S. government itself to be illegitimate, which is why he attacked a federal building while wearing a T-shirt that quoted Thomas Jefferson on the need for liberty to refresh herself in the blood of patriots and tyrants. The fact that there is terrorism in a given spot does not in any sense prove that the government there is normatively illegitimate. But one can generalize and say that sustained and broadly based terrorist movements tend to emerge where a large number of citizens believe that the state denies them their rights and does not represent them. Put another way, for a state to count as democratically legitimate in a descriptive sense, it must succeed in garnering the support of all the major groups of its citizens. (The converse, of course, is not true: a regime can be popular and still democratically illegitimate.) Descriptively speaking, democratic legitimacy, as I use the term here, rests more on the belief that I as a citizen have chosen my government than on the protection of individual rights. There is a reason that, thirty-some years after the heyday of Baader-Meinhof and the Brigate Rosse, what European terror remains is associated with nationalist struggles like those of the Northern Irish or the Basques. Citizens in Northern Ireland and Basques in Spain enjoy basic civil liberties and even vote in elections. To the extent that European terrorist groups possess popular support, that support depends on the belief that their peoples' aspirations to self-determination are justified, and that the governments under which they live were imposed rather than chosen by them.

One can elicit a powerful defensive reaction by suggesting that terrorism may have causes grounded in the perceived illegitimacy of governments. But it is not blaming the victim to observe that people who kill civilians tend to find popular support only when some significant number of others think their cause is just. No normal person likes the intentional killing of noncombatants; so if ordinary people think that civilian deaths are justified in a given instance, it must be that they believe some powerful justification exists for it. No American today is proud of the firebombing of Tokyo, much less of the nuclear attacks on Hiroshima and Nagasaki, yet the fact that these are not generally regarded as a national shame suggests that Americans still consider these operations to have been justified because they hastened the end of the war and thus saved American lives. It follows that we will see popularly supported (and therefore lasting) movements prepared to kill civilians when some large number of people consider such killing justified— and the overthrow of a democratically illegitimate government stands a much better chance of being such a cause than does any grievance against a government chosen by its citizens.

If not only weak states but also democratically illegitimate states breed terror, then we are approaching an alternative version of nation building as a means of justifiable self-protection. The obvious ethical problem with the realist "war on terror" view, according to which states are to be built up regardless of their treatment of their citizens, is that it puts us in the position of employing or colluding in the techniques that states combating terror usually use: torture, summary conviction, and worse. During the Cold War, it was not uncommon for the United States to support anticommunist regimes that did all this and more—a habit that we unfortunately have not kicked. With hindsight, an argument could perhaps be made that this kind of support was justifiable in the light of the overarching goal of defeating communism, a goal that benefited not only Americans but, let us assume, almost everyone in the world. The fact that some authoritarian regimes, like Taiwan and South Korea, eventually morphed into democracies, might serve as an argument for this position—although numerous counterexamples from Latin America and Africa would of course have to be weighed in the balance, alongside even more consequential failures like Iran under the shah.

But even if supporting undemocratic governments may have been justifiable during the Cold War, it is not defensible today. Whether ethically or practically, we cannot now justify supporting repressive governments simply on the ground that we must protect ourselves against terror. This would be doubly true in any instance where, on examination, we concluded that the government in question lacked democratic legitimacy. I am afraid that there are numerous instances today where our present policy of backing autocratic regimes is therefore inescapably wrong, especially in the Muslim world. Where oil enters the picture, so that our support is not only putatively directed at the war against terror but is also aimed to keep the energy supply cheap and steady, our actions are even more reprehensible.[7]

One could defend, however, a strategy of nation building aimed at creating democratically legitimate states that would treat their citizens with dignity and respect, and in which political change could be brought about via party politics, not extralegal violence. States like these would be less likely to give rise to broadly supported terrorist movements that might end up harming us. Our objective in nation building, in other words, would still be the creation of increased global security, including our own security from terror in the United States. Nation building would be the strategy we would pursue in order to achieve this goal: not, let me emphasize, by knocking off illegitimate regimes and then undertaking nation building out of necessity, but using nonviolent means, and re-sorting to force only when there seems to be no other possible route to legitimate government than providing security for what would otherwise become a failed state.

The goal of self-protection is probably the best account of why the United States undertook a nation-building project in Iraq in 2003–4, and why it ought to remain engaged there until some rea-sonably democratic legitimate government has been established. The replacement of Saddam's relatively strong, deterrable state with what will be at best a weak state, vulnerable to terrorist pres-sures, shows pretty definitively that the United States was not pursu-ing any version of the realist war on terror in Iraq—or if it was, the Iraq war must be counted as the most misbegotten and self-contradictory foreign policy blunder in at least a generation. The realist solution to the Saddam problem would have been to replace him with a more pliable general, a strategy the United States self-consciously chose not to pursue. The primary explanation for U.S. pursuit of the extraordinarily difficult—not to say quixotic—task of creating in Iraq a multiparty, federal democracy—one that would be legitimate in the eyes of the overwhelming majority of Iraqis—is that the United States sought to produce an Iraq that will not contribute to increased global insecurity.

Mind you, I do not mean to assume that such a strategy will inevitably, in the long run, make the United States safer than it would be if it were to allow Iraq to decline into chaos and civil war. Possibly the American military presence, continuing well after nominal sovereignty has returned to Iraqis, will end up generating so much ongoing anti-American violence that in fact it would have been wiser from a security standpoint for the United States to have withdrawn at the first sign of trouble. Possibly the attempt to pro-duce a legitimate, elected government will founder on Iraqis' rejec-tion of any entity backed by the United States. Nor do I wish to suggest that self-protective nation building was what motivated the

American invasion in the first place. That choice was the product of several disparate, mutually conflicting strands of thought, some benightedly idealistic, others brutally realist, and almost all based on some misunderstanding of the likely consequences of the invasion in Iraq itself. I mean to propose, rather, that once the invasion had occurred, the regime had collapsed, and the state had ceased to be—not in an orgy of bloody revenge but in an inverted kleptocratic outburst of small-minded looting—creating a democratically legitimate state for purposes of our own self-preservation quickly became the American goal. Some Americans may have arrived in Iraq expecting to re-create Iraqi politics in their own image. But it did not take long on the ground in Baghdad for that kind of grandiose thinking to be replaced by the more immediately self-protective goal of leaving behind a state that would make America safer.

Part of that state-building task involves the rebuilding of the Iraqi nation, a doubtful imagined community nurtured in state violence and looked upon with skepticism by Iraqi Kurds, who make up perhaps a fifth of the population. I shall return to the relationship between state building and nation building later; but for now let me assert only that, whatever the initial goals of regional transformation entertained by some of the war's architects, the objective for the United States in Iraq, at its most ambitious and optimistic, ought to be restricted to creating a reasonably just and democratic state that is acceptable to Iraqis.

A glance at the halfheartedness of what Michael Ignatieff has called the "lite" nation-building efforts in Bosnia, Kosovo, and Afghanistan[8] might well lead a skeptic to wonder how anyone could entertain the view that any American administration would actually commit itself to the goal of producing democracy in Iraq. The tendency of the United States, and indeed of the United Nations and its member states, has been to settle for the dampening of violence, not to devote to nation building the resources or time that would be needed for it to succeed. But let me remind you that this nation-building goal ought to be understood in wholly self-protective terms. Needless to say, no one's motivations are simple in the world of foreign policy. Do not take me to be saying that, for any one individual in the U.S. government, we could pin down the precise objective of building a serviceable democracy in Iraq. There are those in the government (as outside) who would withdraw at a moment's notice if they could, and others who seek regional domination without regard to internal legitimacy.

All I mean to argue is that the most defensible account of our nation-building policies in Iraq in 2003–4, and the standard to which future U.S. efforts should be held, is the production of a basically legitimate, functioning democracy there. Such a democracy would be desirable from the American perspective because it would promote the stability and legitimacy of the Iraqi government and consequently protect the United States against terror. Nonstate violence, rare under Saddam, has already begun in Iraq in earnest, and it may well spill over to the continental United States directly if no legitimate state emerges in Iraq. Now that the can of worms has been opened—to say nothing of the can of whup-ass—the only way to get it closed is a government that Iraqis consider democratically legitimate. Or if you prefer the biblical image to the vernacular one, the cup of wrath has passed to Iraq and will not cease to be drunk until justice shall reign in that land.

At this point, having introduced the possibility that the United States could be understood to have pursued nation building in Iraq for self-protective reasons, in the hope of reducing the likelihood of Iraq-inspired terrorism by constructing a legitimate democracy there, I want to consider the criticism that this vision of nation building is purely instrumentalist. Perhaps you will agree with me that the approach I have characterized as the realist war on terror is both unwise and ethically unsustainable because of its support for unjust regimes. But this does not mean that the alternative I have sketched satisfies the demands of ethics, either. Certainly if we were to apply a moral calculus that called on us to treat nations or their citizens as ends rather than means, the instrumentalism of self-protective nation building would look questionable. After all, according to my hypothesis, the United States has pursued nation building in Iraq not because of any inherent concern for the Iraqi people but primarily to serve its own interests in security. The problem, then, seems to be one of moral motivation.

There is a prominent strain of moral theory, sometimes applied to international affairs by specialists and laypeople alike, that condemns this sort of instrumentalism. One hears the challenge put bluntly, if effectively, in the Middle East, in Europe, and indeed in Greenwich Village: how can American nation building in Iraq be morally acceptable if it is designed to serve U.S. interests? With its Kantian overtones, this argument can be associated with what Weber called the ethic of conscience.[9] It demands that we act morally, or not at all. This argument has been used to demand an immediate withdrawal of American troops and personnel from Iraq, but its consequences are more far-reaching. In terms that are gaining real purchase around the globe, this argument purports to subject the international behavior of powerful nations to a strict moral test akin to a requirement of altruism—and for this reason, if for no other, it deserves serious consideration and reply.[10]

Moral discourse has, let me emphasize, an important place in thinking about nation building. What is more, the tensions between American and Iraqi interests in the nation-building project in Iraq are and have been real, and must be carefully addressed in ethical terms. Indeed, I shall be arguing in the next chapter that in choosing the means by which to effectuate its policies in an occupied country like Iraq, the nation builder must guard against placing its own interests ahead of those of the people under occupation. When it comes to our motives in setting objectives, however, I want to propose that an ethic requiring us to define our objectives without treating others' interests instrumentally asks too much in the context of international action. It should be sufficient, I want to argue, if our objectives *coincide* with the interests of other peoples or nations, and if we adopt appropriate means to achieve them. Our objectives themselves need not be motivated by anything other than our own needs.

In ordinary individual moral terms, this attitude toward motivation in the setting of objectives may sound too modest. Perhaps I am under a duty to be moved by the interests of other people—query *which* other people?—when I set my life goals.[11] But I think it is possible to argue, even in the individual context, that I am not bound to think of others when I specify what counts as a good life for myself, *so long as my goals coincide with or at least do not conflict with the interests of other people*. If I take as my life plan the oppression of others, the morally problematic aspect of this decision is obviously that it does not coincide with the interests of the people I plan to oppress. If I take it as my selfish objective to play professional basketball, this goal may turn out to be unattainable, but it is not morally objectionable so long as it does not require me to harm others to do so.

I do not insist, however, that this point holds morally for the ordinary individual. All I must argue to show that self-protective nation building may be morally defensible is that when *governments* form their objectives, it is enough that those objectives coincide with the interests of other nations and are implemented through morally permissible means. Government objectives are complicated things, as I mentioned earlier in discussing the reasons we undertook the Iraq war in the first place. They grow out of multiple individual and collective motives, some of which will turn out to be mutually contradictory. Through a well-established logical anomaly that goes back to Condorcet, we know that group decisions sometimes do not reflect the ordered preferences of any of the decision makers.[12] In that case, what exactly count as the group's objectives?

This puzzle may not be susceptible of an easy solution, and I do not propose one here.[13] Nonetheless I think we can suggest that, with all the complex factors at play in group decisions, it is unrealistic to expect that the overlapping goals on which a big group like a government converges be motivated by concern for the interest of persons who are not members of the collective.

Another way of putting this descriptive point would be to say that, charged with the already difficult task of forming coherent goals despite the differing desires and interests of its own citizens, a government is very unlikely to take on the further obligation of defining its goals based on the interests of noncitizens. Governments, or at least legitimate governments, exist in any case to coordinate the needs and desires of some specified group of people, namely, the citizens. The purpose of a world government would require it to consider everyone's interests; but the purpose of a national government is to facilitate goal formation based on the interests of its own citizens.

Although it would be mistaken to derive a theory of what kinds of government action are morally justifiable from a description of what governments actually do, we can draw on the reality of the way governments coordinate citizens' goals in order to ascertain whether we think our governments' ordinary mechanisms of goal formation are morally defensible. If we think that it is morally acceptable to form national governments, which coordinate only their citizens' interests, and that we are not under a moral obligation to create a world government that would be responsible to the interests of all persons everywhere, then it follows that we must believe it is acceptable for a government to form goals based on the interests of its citizens. An analogy can be drawn to the context of local or state government: my city or my state gives tax incentives to companies or sports franchises in the hope of luring them to our locale, not to other municipalities with which it is competing. Ordinarily, we seem to think this course of action is acceptable, even though it clearly involves placing our own goals in, say, economic development, above the goals of our neighbors. Some moral theorist might object that, strictly speaking, we are wrong to favor our own goals over those of other persons separated from us by some arbitrary border. But such a moral position, which has much in common with the view that we are wrong to value our relatives or friends ahead of strangers, seems too disconnected from the moral intuitions that grow out of ordinary experience to be convincing.

Of course, saying government need not be motivated by the interests of noncitizens in forming goals does not mean that government is not subject to some constraints in the activity of goal formation. I do not want my argument to prove too much. If we citizens individually would be unjustified in defining goals that we can achieve only by wronging other people, we cannot avoid the problem merely by banding together into a government and then setting goals that inherently involve injustice toward third parties. Oppression of others, for example, does not suddenly become justifiable simply because we all agree to our government's pursuing oppressive goals. So there will be limits to the goals we can permissibly form—specifically, the limits imposed by the obligation not to do injustice. The constraints, though, do not alter the basic claim that our *motivation* in forming goals may permissibly be selfish.

Defining what counts as injustice toward others in the international sphere lies outside the scope of my argument in this chapter. All we are looking for is an accessible account of whether the goal of self-protective nation building might be justified even though it is motivated by the interests of the nation builder. For our purposes, it should be enough to conclude that, at a minimum, the government may permissibly set its goals on the basis of its own citizens' interests *whenever those goals do not fundamentally conflict with the interests of people whom the government does not represent.* A fuller moral account would require us to specify more. Under the right conditions, we might well be permitted to set objectives that do conflict with others' interests. Moreover, the means we employ must also satisfy some moral conditions, which I will discuss in the next chapter. But for now this loosely Millian minimal principle should serve our purpose.

The key claim for applying this principle to our problem is that self-protective nation building does not conflict with the interests of the peoples whose nations are to be built. In fact, I want to assert, living under a democratically legitimate government that respects basic rights coincides with a people's interests.[14] For this reason, self-protective nation building can be morally justifiable despite the fact that it proceeds from motives of the protective self-interest of the state or states doing the building.

To see why, look back to the nation-building projects in Germany and Japan, undertaken not in the interests of the German or Japanese people—for whom Americans in 1945 felt little but hatred—but rather with the goal of creating strong allies to fight communism. These instances of nation building were surely morally justified, even though they were wholly instrumental from the U.S. perspective, because they coincided with German and Japanese interests in becoming prosperous.[15] There were plenty of details of these reconstructions that the Germans and Japanese would not have chosen for themselves, of course. Demilitarization, accomplished constitutionally in both countries, was an American-imposed demand. In fact, in its entirety, nation building in Germany and Japan was structured as an offer that the occupied peoples could not refuse. I mean that phrase in its classic, Coppolan sense: a significant upside benefit for cooperation coupled with a coercive threat to discourage defection.

So by saying that nation building coincided with the interests of occupied Germany and Japan, I do not mean to suggest that the Germans or the Japanese got to set the agenda. They did not; the United States did. Nor do I mean to suggest that the mechanisms whereby the interests of Iraqis should be taken into account can be derived from the cases of Germany and Japan. The fact that these nations had been aggressors vis-à-vis the United States meant that the latter was entitled to take longer implementing true participatory mechanisms through which the occupied peoples could express their political desires. All I want to show is that the goals of nation building may plausibly be driven by the motives of the occupier, so long as those goals coincide with the interests of the occupied.

The ethical problem of whether and how moral motivation matters is a deep one, recurring in international affairs generally.[16] Strong nations, like powerful people, have a tendency to act in what they themselves define as their own self-interest; and any serious theory of ethics in international affairs must acknowledge and take account of this reality. I am trying to suggest here a direction worth exploring in addressing this general problem, which is particularly acute when it comes to occupation. Broadly, I believe an adequate ethical theory of international relations can accept nations' choice and desire to define their objectives in terms of what they believe is right for their own citizens—so long as the theory also offers constraints on how those objectives may justifiably be put into practice. The only way such ethical constraints will have any real-world bite, of course, is if the citizens and governments of powerful countries are actually prepared to take them seriously. But this does not seem impossible, if the argument is made effectively. The recent examples of U.S. intervention in Bosnia and Kosovo suggest a public willingness to do the right thing even when national security is not obviously in jeopardy; and at the individual level, many people often behave morally even at some personal cost.

It should be an attractive feature of my account of selfish motivation in goal specification that it corresponds to a possible reality. It is, I think, inevitable that governments will form goals on the basis of what they take to be the interests of their citizens; but it is not inevitable that the implementation of those goals must therefore be unethical. Constraints on how goals are brought about can realistically derive from the ethical and moral principles that citizens make their own. In these chapters, therefore, when I advocate a particular position as ethically attractive, I am simultaneously proposing that we as citizens take it on board as relevant to the way we act as a nation.

It is, in other words, a virtue of an ethical approach to be capable of shaping discourse and decisions in the world of actual politics. For a politician to be able to convince the American people that nation building in Iraq is worth pursuing and should not be abandoned at the first signs of trouble, he or she must be able to articulate some goals that serve American security interests. Otherwise, whatever we may conclude about the duties we owe Iraq now that we have destroyed the Iraqis' government and cast their national future into uncertainty, voices in the American political sphere calling for withdrawal regardless of consequences may well be allowed to prevail. If we insist that any argument for nation building, or indeed other international action, depends upon putting aside Americans' motivated interests in their own security, the consequence will certainly be inaction.

"Good!" I can almost hear some readers saying. "A little more inaction is just what we need in the international sphere to help us avoid getting into messes like the one in Iraq." Those who feel this way might prefer a more stringent moral check on our motives in goal definition, precisely because we will do less if we have to satisfy a high standard of forming our objectives based on more than our own interests. Under that standard, we will often simply be unable to reach consensus; and indecision will produce inaction.

No doubt, the Hippocratic oath has something to contribute to an enlightened foreign policy.[17] Doing no harm is an intuitively appealing principle, and so it might sound attractive to set the moral standard for action so high that we will rarely if ever reach it. But it is also a dangerous principle when we are confronting a situation in which inaction is itself a form of action; where some decisive actions have already been taken by us or by others, and we are called upon to react to them. It is already too late to write upon a blank slate in Iraq. Imposing a high bar to action after the fact will not reverse the decision to invade. Happily, it will not bring Saddam back; but whether we like it or not, it also cannot assure the safety or well-being of the Iraqis themselves. There are worse things than totalitarianism, as we have learned in places like Somalia and Sierra Leone, and we must ensure that Iraq does not head further in that anarchic direction. We need *some* model for how to proceed in a place like Iraq—and if we pose a moral standard that cannot be satisfied in practice, we can expect to hear the familiar argument that morality should be irrelevant to our foreign policy.

I am not suggesting that moral principle should be compromised just so that ethics can play a role in our foreign policy debates. But I do mean to argue that absolutist morality is out of place in situations where we are never starting from scratch, and are embedded in a set of past decisions and evolving conditions that call for us to take a position and act upon it. What we need is an ethic that acknowledges both the politically immovable impulse to serve national security and also the moral principles that most, or perhaps nearly all, Americans would be willing to adopt if those principles were put to the public clearly and directly. Such an approach will have something in common with Weber's ethic of responsibility, which concerns itself with the foreseeable consequences of action and refuses to take refuge in moral principles that are disconnected from results in the real world.[18] It will be above all a practical ethic, one admitting that even if the invasion of Iraq was unwise or immoral, we are still stuck with its actual consequences.

In the case of Iraq, and indeed other recent nation-building projects, the emerging political reality is that it is actually rather easier to motivate Americans to support an invasion—however expensive—than it is to convince them to sustain nation building in the aftermath of military action. Haiti is a prominent example. The 1994 U.S. invasion was at the last moment unopposed, and within two years the last U.S. troops were gone. A decade later—during which little was done in the way of providing support for democratic institutions or economic development—conditions were no better than they had been when President Clinton authorized the use of force to return the democratically elected Bertrand Aristide to power;[19] and when in spring 2004 President Bush declined to send troops to save Aristide from yet another coup, Aristide ended up in exile, exactly where he would have been had Clinton never acted.

The case of Afghanistan is perhaps even more troubling. There, a constitutional process produced a document that embodies the ideals of Islamic democracy; and yet the state remains unconsolidated, in large part because of U.S. unwillingness to devote the resources that would be necessary for political centralization and economic development. About the best thing in economic terms that happened to Afghans after the fall of the Taliban was the restoration of the illegal heroin trade to world-leader levels. You can bet that Afghanistan will remain outside American national consciousness until that country reemerges as a staging ground for terrorism.[20]

These examples demonstrate why those who care about the ethical consequences of American action need to develop a model for public discussion that allows room for the self-interest of security while simultaneously charting duties and obligations. Otherwise, Iraq could potentially go the way of Afghanistan—a quasi-feudal division of power among various elites, with the fissures in the political structure barely concealed under an attractive paper constitution. That arrangement would, in the long run, prove unstable, with disastrous consequences in both moral and practical senses. Total state collapse would not be impossible. So while a general theory should not be devised just to fit the particular facts of one case, it is also true that whatever view we develop to guide our thinking about nation building should be capable of withstanding the reality check of whether it will work in Iraq or in other, future cases.

The need for a serious, ethically grounded discussion is not only ends-oriented, in the sense that without it there will always be pressure to cut and run. Such a discussion is necessary to sustain the goal of actually *being ethical*. As events on the ground develop, we will need to regain our ethical bearings to figure out what course to pursue. Our ethical responsibilities cannot fluctuate with the news cycle; but neither can we ignore profound changes as they occur. An ethical response to real-world events does not produce reflective equilibrium, except briefly. The best we can hope for is keeping our ship afloat, and headed in the right direction.

The attempt to explain and justify nation building in the post–Cold War environment, and especially in Iraq, naturally calls up the historical perspective of the nation-building rhetoric and efforts of the post–World War I era. Indeed, the arguments to this point might be loosely associated with the species of "enlightened self-interest" ordinarily attributed to Woodrow Wilson. But isn't this possibility something to worry about? After all, Wilsonianism had its crack at nation building in the Middle East in general, and Iraq in particular—and that approach was a spectacular failure. To be sure, it did not appear so as late as the middle of the 1930s. One obscure book on the history and ethnic configuration of Iraq, published in 1935,[21] which I came across while preparing for my own first trip to Iraq, proudly declared on its first page that Iraq had emerged as a "democratic state" as a consequence of the Wilson-drafted Article 22 of the Covenant of the League of Nations and its successful execution by Great Britain during the period of British mandatory rule. But as every Iraqi schoolchild knows, the British-backed monarchy did not turn out to be a successful democracy. It struggled on until 1958 as a constitutional monarchy prone to constant governmental flux[22] before giving way to a revolution that itself was followed in quick succession by half a dozen changes in power until Saddam emerged as the undisputed heavyweight champion in 1979. Haven't we been down this road before?

Readers of David Fromkin's provocative and popular *A Peace to End All Peace*[23] have learned to blame the region's problems on the thinly disguised colonial motivations of the British and French, which—though costumed in the cloak of mandate and nation building—were more like the last, pathetic moves in the great game of world power that these empires were playing to a stalemate. In the early days of the 2003 occupation, the historian Toby Dodge produced a monograph criticizing the British nation-building strategy in Iraq, and warning that the Americans were on the verge of repeating it, with comparably disastrous results.[24] The general argument that might be derived from such books is that nation building is a fool's game, especially in artificial countries ginned up to serve colonizers and subsequently preserved by sword and poison gas. With respect to Iraq, goes the claim, the Americans were doubly foolish: foolish morally in purporting to take up the white man's burden in a world where such "civilizing" or democratizing ideals are anachronistic at best; and foolish practically for thinking that they could pick up a burden which the British put down gladly seventy years earlier, and carry it to the finish line.

These arguments need to be taken very seriously, both with respect to the moral implications of a nation-building strategy that may be characterized as neocolonial or neoimperial, and with respect to the practical charge that it is pointless to try to build a nation in Iraq, much less a democratic nation, where others have tried and failed. It was sometimes difficult to avoid the powerful sense of the eternal return in Iraqi affairs in 2003–4. Certainly the triumphant tone of the 1935 declaration that democracy had been achieved in Iraq haunted me during my time in Baghdad, especially when I was listening to the Coalition's spokespeople describing the handpicked Governing Council or the rather more rough-and-ready local councils as the most "democratic" governing bodies in the region. The United States made mistakes in Iraq that were reminiscent of those made by the British, and in our own supremely naive American way, we seemed to believe both that we were morally purer than our predecessors and that we knew better what we were doing.

The former might conceivably have been true—though I very much doubt it—but the latter was certainly false. The number of Americans who spoke Arabic in the Coalition Provisional Authority was shamefully, shockingly low.[25] Many of the best State Department regional experts never set foot in Iraq during the CPA's tenure, either because internal administration politics excluded war skeptics from service in Baghdad or because, mindful of their careers, they did not want to touch Iraq with a ten-foot pole. We did not have a well-developed theory of how best to produce legitimate democracy in Iraq. Indeed, famously, when the war began, we did not even have a plan.

It therefore makes sense to tackle the question whether there was ever any reasonable prospect of accomplishing the objective that I have sketched: the facilitation of a legitimate, basically democratic government in Iraq that would respect its citizens' rights and, not coincidentally, produce the stability and legitimacy needed to avoid insurrection and terrorism. An unachievable nation-building project would probably have been immoral if we knew it to be doomed from the start, but immorality would be the least of our worries if that were the case. Could it be done? And if we think the answer is yes, why should the United States—with or without the UN's assistance—succeed where the British and the League of Nations had failed?

I have spent numerous sleepless nights worrying about this question, some of them on the floor of the kitchen of the Republican Palace in Baghdad. The architectural vicissitudes of that structure reveal something of the nature of the problem. The core of the building is a modest-sized office palace (in Baghdad one learned to distinguish office palaces from residential palaces), roughly rectangular in shape, with a low Palladian dome and a small rotunda beneath it. This was built under King Feisal—during the period of British tutelage—for official functions and administrative operations, and it continued to be used in the same way during the period after 1958, when it was named the Republican Palace in honor of the new form of government that accompanied the revolution.

After Saddam came to dominate Iraqi politics absolutely in 1979, the building sprouted two absurdly long wings, all out of proportion to the central core. The wings swept outward so that the structure came to resemble a kind of pterodactyl, built for flight with a foreshortened body that seemed almost an afterthought. The bricks for the additions were individually stamped with Saddam's monogram, after the manner of the Babylonian emperors who wanted posterity to know their names. But these wings, decorated in what can only be described as pseudo-Andalusian dictator rococo, were not enough for Saddam. At four points along the two wings, he erected enormous facsimiles of his head, each roughly five times the height of a man. The heads were clad in helmets that looked a bit like a combination of a Prussian *Pickelhaube* and an Arab *kaffiyeh*. The mustaches alone must have been ten feet across and three or four feet high. Bizarre and horrifying at once, the heads exemplified the self-replicating character of Saddamist rule: one head was not enough. There must be doubles, triples, quadruples.

The heads are gone, gingerly removed in a proceeding that made the front page of the *New York Times*. Until June 28, 2004, the building functioned as the headquarters of the occupation administration, at which time it was magically transformed into an annex of the U.S. embassy to the nominally sovereign Iraqi government. Yet through the occupation, and beyond, the palace remained a chaos of bricolage, army cots interspersed with computers, satellite dishes, and seemingly endless stacks of Meals Ready to Eat, each a five-thousand-calorie carbohydrate bomb designed to sustain a man marching twenty miles with a one-hundred-pound pack on his back.[26]

The mess in the Republican Palace suggests the mixed results of the occupation's ad hoc, improvisational efforts to transform the edifice of the Baʿthist state—itself built on the serviceable structure of the postcolonial Iraqi monarchy—into a thing of the people. The Republican Palace has not yet earned its name, unless one takes it ironically, in the partisan American sense. The Coalition did remove the heads, as it were, and that is not a trivial thing. Saddam actually was imprisoned, and he actually never will reassert control, to the amazement of a generation of Iraqis who had known no other ruler. In his place, however, there emerged a nascent Iraqi politics characterized mostly by uncertainty and violence. Until elections could be held—and during the period of occupation, they were not—any assessment of Iraqi public opinion was inevitably based on imperfect polling and informed speculation. The occupation authorities measured an ayatollah's influence by the reaction of politicians after his pronouncements, and secondarily by the number of people he could put on the streets to chant his slogans. About the only thing of which the CPA could be certain was that ordinary Kurds—among the worst treated of Wilson's protégés—preferred independence to autonomy, and that an armed force of between fifty and seventy-five thousand *pesh merga* would ensure that they got at least the latter.

Yet despite this unpromising situation, and a host of further risks too lengthy and dynamic to enumerate exhaustively, it remained possible throughout the occupation period that nation building could yield acceptable results. Despite its hodgepodge character as a state agglomerated by the British out of three Ottoman provinces, Iraq did not, during the period of occupation, split into its constituent parts. Inspired by the proximity of a hostile and suspicious

Turkey, the Kurdish leadership took the position that its bread was, for the time being at least, buttered on the side of federalism, not independence. For the most part, ordinary Kurds proved willing to go along with this plan, despite a strong attachment to the ideal of independence. Naturally the Kurds played hardball in constitutional negotiations, as they will continue to do so long as the constitutional process lasts. Every Iraqi Kurd I have ever met says that Kurdistan must have and keep the de facto option of seceding if the rest of the country treats it unjustly or collapses. Jalal Talabani, leader of the Patriotic Union of Kurdistan, said as much during negotiations over the Transitional Administrative Law (TAL) that was signed on March 8, 2004. It is also entirely reasonable to think that many Kurds saw and still see regional autonomy as a stepping-stone to full independence, to be achieved should Turkey realize it has more to gain than to lose from the existence of a Kurdish buffer state between its European Unionist aspirations and Iraqi violence. For the medium term, though, the Kurdish leadership has opted to be part of Iraq—and if this admittedly delicate arrangement turns out to be satisfactory, they will remain in for the foreseeable future.

For now, in any case, as during the occupation period, the breakup of the country could not be accomplished without bloodshed. Neither Kurds nor Sunnis are prepared to give up Kirkuk without a fight, as much for its massive oil field as for its sentimental value. Baghdad, for that matter, is a city of some 5 or 6 million—roughly a dozen times the size of Sarajevo—with a mixed population of Sunnis, Shi'is, and Kurds whose relationship has been uneasy. In a civil war, the imbricated populations could be at each other's throats, with results too horrifying to imagine.

Meanwhile the clerics—who, in the preelection period, spoke almost exclusively for Iraq's Shi'i Muslims—emerged as the loudest voices in the country calling for electoral democracy. Most disclaimed an interest in running Iraq along the lines of what they consider the failed Iranian model; but of course, as leaders of a majority, they called for elections to ensure that the Shiʿa would not be marginalized as they had been throughout Iraqi political history. The Shiʿis who seem to have been most politically successful are Islamic democrats, men like Ibrahim Jaʿfari of the Islamic Daʿwa Party, who profess the compatibility of Islam and democratic rights and values. They called not for theocracy but for limited constitutional government that would protect individual rights and tolerate religious difference. Whether in office they will make good on these promises cannot be guaranteed; but as much might be said of any politician in a new democracy whose institutions are not yet firmly established.[27]

Ayatollah ʿAli Sistani emerged as the most prominent spokesman for electoral democracy in Iraq. A glance at his metamorphosis— from a respected cleric, known mostly for his view that mullahs should not intervene in politics, into a sophisticated player conducting, in essence, multilateral negotiations among himself, the secretary general of the United Nations, and the president of the United States—should reveal something about the prospects for democracy in Iraq. His strategy from the outset was one of caution. With just two or three extremely well-timed, carefully framed public statements in a period of six months, he created the impression of capturing the allegiance of millions of Shiʿis and as a result managed to become a figure whom no one could afford to ignore, and who played the most significant individual role in Iraqi politics during the period of occupation.

When Saddam fell, Sistani was first among equals in the leadership of the *hawza* of Najaf, a kind of commission of roughly a thousand Shiʿi clerics who gain their authority over the community's religious affairs through advanced Islamic legal study and personal piety. There is no obvious or easy analogy for the *hawza*, which lacks the wealth and global reach of the Holy See; but perhaps it could be said that the *hawza* is a cross between the Roman curia and a distinguished faculty of arts and sciences in a major research university. Najaf competes with Qom for influence in the Shiʿi world, and the status of the thousand-year-old *hawza* of Najaf is closely connected to this competition.[28]

Advancement within the clerical hierarchy is not based on constituencies that are easily transferable into broader political power. If it were, it would have been very difficult for Sistani, an Iranian by birth, to reach its apex. Sistani's Persian-accented Arabic was not suitable for rousing Iraqi audiences—and let us recall that Iraq's Shiʿis fought for Iraq, not Iran, during the bitter war between the two countries. Nor was Sistani exceptional in being a foreigner who rose within the *hawza*: of the four senior members at the time Saddam fell, there was also an Afghani and a Pakistani. So while the *hawza* certainly has its own complex internal politics, which exist in some relation to the broader Shiʿi community, Sistani's political experience was not of the national or international variety. The only politics with which he had any experience was the small-group variety, in which representativeness counted for little, but intelligence, judgment, and getting things right counted for a lot.

Acting through intermediaries, the United States initially sought a statement from Sistani calling for cooperation with occupation forces. Sistani declined even to meet with U.S. officials, citing his traditional practice and widely recognized view that clerics should stay out of politics. He made it clear, however, that he also would not condemn the occupation. For a man who had survived Saddam's regime—as more activist Shiʿi clerics had not—this was simply prudence and a continuation of his previous strategy. It is possible that Sistani read the American request as a sign that Shiʿi power was going to grow under U.S. occupation. Certainly Saddam had never demanded or asked for Sistani's blessing, because doing so would have implicitly acknowledged some need for legitimation from outside the state structure, a sure sign of political weakness. But in any case, Sistani cautiously adopted a wait-and-see strategy, and the Americans had to be satisfied with that.

At the same time he was declining to take a stand on national politics, Sistani had to fend off challenges to the authority of the *hawza* coming from two different directions. The more serious threat, from his perspective, came from Ayatollah Muhammad Bakr al-Hakim, who had spent the previous decade in Iran as the leader of an exiled political organization with the alarming name "Supreme Council for Islamic Revolution in Iraq" (SCIRI), often referred to by the first word of its Arabic name as "the *majlis*" (council). The *majlis* was an Iranian creation with its own militia, the Badr Brigades, some ten thousand strong. Muhammad Bakr al-Hakim was a certified scholar, an ayatollah himself, even if not quite in Sistani's league. But he was primarily a professional politician, which Sistani assuredly was not. Bakr al-Hakim was tempered by long experience seeking support in the back rooms of Iranian politics, an environment of mind-boggling complexity where the mullahs and the government were profoundly interlocked, and Iraqi affairs were pieces in a game that would make chess look simple.[29]

In May 2003, Bakr al-Hakim staged a triumphant return to Iraq, and thousands of Shi'is turned out to escort him from the border to the holy cities of Najaf and Karbala. The *majlis* had been active in exile politics and in close contact with the United States. After some hesitation, it chose to join the Governing Council, cementing those relations further and presenting itself to the Coalition as the true representative of the Iraqi Shi'a. Bakr al-Hakim bid fair to become the major clerical figure in the country just by coming home.

Sistani avoided direct confrontation. His supporters quietly emphasized the superiority of his scholarship and his apolitical stance. Then in July 2003, Bakr al-Hakim was assassinated by a car bomb as he left the shrine of Imam ʿAli in Najaf. The attack seemed to have come from Sunni quarters—it was unlikely that Shi'is would have profaned the holiest spot for their denomination, killing as many as one hundred bystanders in the process.[30] It left Bakr al-Hakim's academically undistinguished younger brother, ʿAbdul ᶜAziz, as the head of the *majlis*; and it thereby effectively removed the *majlis* as a threat to Sistani's authority, because ᶜAbdul ᶜAziz, who was not an ayatollah himself, had to defer to Sistani in order to maintain clerical legitimacy. Sistani's political prominence, then, was in part accidental; he would never have gained the influence that he did if Ayatollah Muhammad Bakr al-Hakim had remained alive.

That left only the young mullah Muqtada Sadr to challenge the *hawza*. To Western eyes, Muqtada was a revolutionary straight from central casting. Son of the martyred grand ayatollah whom Sistani had succeeded, he called loudly for clerical rule on the Iranian model and very quickly became popular in the poorest Shiᶜi slums of Baghdad. Just thirty-two himself, and surrounded by a group of angry and ambitious young clerics, Muqtada aimed to put the fear of God into the local population by spreading the warning that women without head scarves, sellers of alcohol, and cinema operators would be severely punished by vigilantes. Muqtada denounced the occupation from its outset and even went so far at one point as to announce, rather optimistically, the creation of his own government. Despite growing concern about Muqtada within the CPA, Sistani remained unfazed, adopting a strategy of ignoring the upstart while emphasizing to his own community that Shiᶜi clerical authority could be exercised only by permission of the *hawza*. When Muqtada's boys tried to set up their own courts in the chaos of the postwar months, Sistani's supporters spread the word to the Shiᶜi community that these were unauthorized and illegitimate. This was a classic defense by institutional authority against incipient charismatic appeal.[31]

Sistani's strategy worked—and for a time, the CPA played along, declining to arrest Muqtada despite his provocations. By autumn 2003, Muqtada seemed to have faded. His resurgence in spring 2004 was largely a product of the botched CPA attempts to close his newspaper and arrest him, both of which reestablished his fading credibility. His small militia enhanced its prestige by a series of take-overs of police stations and municipal buildings in southern Iraq. This required Sistani, through intermediaries, to undertake to nego-tiate their withdrawal, which could be accomplished only at the cost of giving some recognition to Muqtada; but Sistani remained the more important power player.

Sistani's first and critical political move, though, had come in the summer of 2003. In a one-paragraph *fatwa*, he reacted to (accurate) reports that the CPA planned for the Iraqi constitution to be drafted by a constitutional drafting body to be chosen by a selection pro-cess, not by direct elections. The *fatwa* was pure democratic theory, with nary a reference to Islamic legal texts. It said simply that "those forces" (the Coalition, named by a circumlocution to avoid giving it either recognition or offense) had no authority to write a constitu-tion for Iraq. There must be elections for the constitution-drafting body, so that the constitution would reflect the social values and religious beliefs of the Iraqi people.[32] Couched thus generally, the *fatwa* was designed to appeal not only to religiously observant Shi'is but to all Iraqis. Its conclusion and its reasoning were, indeed, essen-tially indistinguishable from those of any competent international lawyer. Within the CPA, such views had been privately expressed by international lawyers from a variety of countries, experienced in nation building elsewhere, who assumed the Iraqi constitution could be written only by an elected constituent assembly, and were appalled by any suggestions to the contrary.

It took some time for the impact of the *fatwa* to be fully felt by the CPA, which had charged the Governing Council to name a preparatory committee to investigate the possibilities for creating a constitution-drafting body. The preparatory committee found itself completely constrained by the existence of the *fatwa*. Twenty-four of its twenty-five members eventually traveled en masse to Najaf for an audience with Sistani. They left unanimous in their certainty that his argument could not be refuted. The preparatory committee then dissolved without reporting back to the Governing Council. Sistani was now dictating policy.

In part as a reaction to the Governing Council's inability to recommend a strategy for constitution writing without elections, Washington, acting through the CPA, changed course. In November 2003 the CPA proposed that, to satisfy Sistani, the constitution would indeed eventually be written by an elected constituent assembly. Until that could happen, the country would be governed, starting on June 30, 2004, by a transitional national assembly to be selected by caucuses, rather than direct elections. This plan appeared to satisfy the letter of Sistani's *fatwa* but entirely missed the spirit, which was for electoral democracy, not appointed rulers. In late 2003, a month after the CPA and the Governing Council had formally agreed to this two-tiered plan, Sistani made a statement expressing his disapproval of any process other than elections to choose even the interim government. He left open the possibility that elections by June 30, 2004, might not be possible—and his staff indicated that the views of the secretary general on this question would be appreciated. That sent Ambassador Bremer back to Washington and thence to Turtle Bay, accompanied by nine members of the Governing Council, to meet with Secretary General Kofi Annan. Ayatollah Sistani had done what Tony Blair could not: he had brought the United States to the United Nations, hat in hand, seeking its involvement in nation building in Iraq.

How did Sistani do it? He combined a preexistent institutional authority with a single, simple, and easily defended demand: if this is to be a democracy, where are the elections? It was almost unnecessary for Sistani's supporters to stage a 100,000-person march in Baghdad, as they did in late January 2004, to underscore the point that the overwhelming majority of Iraqi Shiʿis—and not a few Sunnis—could agree that Iraqis wanted to choose their own leaders, not have leaders thrust upon them by some indirect process in which the United States would have disproportionate control.

Sistani also took his time. Almost every other would-be politician in Iraq, whether returning from exile or domestically grown, moved too fast, too aggressively, trying to gain a foothold in the postwar environment. The politicians' belief, plausibly enough, was that it was now or never: almost no new political figure in Iraq had any name recognition. As a consequence of thrusting themselves forward, most of the aspiring Iraqi political class succeeded only in revealing the impossibility of jumping from political unknown to mobilizer of large constituencies. Political power in Iraq, as anywhere else, must be built one step at a time, according to the rules of the local game. There are no shortcuts, or at least no obvious ones. The overambitious attempts of the returnee politicians seemed particularly ineffective because they were closely connected to the wavering and unstable policies for the transfer of power proposed by the CPA.

In Iraq's extraordinary preconstitutional moment, Sistani was prepared to put aside his traditional political quiescence—the habit and practice of a lifetime. But knowing that his influence derived from his being above ordinary politics, and careful not to lower his stature, Sistani stepped gingerly when it came to particular political problems. In the negotiations leading to the Transitional Administrative Law, Sistani focused once again on high-level principles of majoritarianism, challenging the proposal of a minority regional veto of a final constitution, then grudgingly agreeing to the provision's appearing in the TAL, subject to subsequent renegotiation. When the UN Security Council had the opportunity to endorse the TAL, Sistani successfully opposed their doing so, on the same majoritarian grounds.

In the final analysis, the Shiʿa will inevitably be a majority in a democratic Iraq. Although elections may be vulnerable to terrorist attack, they will have to happen sometime. So Sistani, one can predict with confidence, will get his way. Eventually there will be national elections for a transitional government in Iraq.[33] The really difficult and important question concerns what will happen once elections for the transitional government and constituent assembly occur. What sort of government and institutions will emerge? Do they have a chance of becoming durable?

This brings us to the all-important question of Iraq's Sunni Arabs and their place in Iraq's future. Sunni Arabs only gradually began to accept the reality that they were going to be a minority in the new Iraq, and the stepwise growth of the insurgency during the occupation period owed much to this state of denial. In the formal terms favored by the game theorists who model democratization, some nontrivial number of Sunnis seemed to believe that the summed costs and benefits to them of subverting the emergence of a democratic government in Iraq outweighed the costs and benefits of entering into a democratic state in which they feared becoming permanent losers.[34] Some certainly believed that if they killed enough Americans, the U.S. occupiers would leave, in which case they might still have some chance of reestablishing Sunni dominance. (Possibly, some Sunnis even believed that long-term anarchy would be preferable to living under Shi'i domination.) There is also a more nuanced version of this strategic view: perhaps killing Americans would not alone break U.S. resolve; but by killing Iraqi police and disrupting the possibilities of transition, the insurgents might be able to delay the emergence of a state with the power to enforce the laws. They could delay that process long enough for the United States to run out of patience and decide it was too costly to remain as an occupier. This scenario would also result in eventual American withdrawal, opening the door for the Sunnis to reassert control.

The reasons to believe that calculations like these were present in at least the leadership of the insurgency are the care with which targets were chosen, and the relative paucity of Islamist, as opposed to nationalist, rhetoric among those Iraqis who sympathized with the resisters during most of the year of occupation. The foreign Sunni Islamists (especially Yemenis) who were in Iraq during the occupation period to fight a different sort of suicidal jihad were pursuing a different agenda, with which fewer Iraqis seemed to have sympathy. That could change, of course. The Palestinian resistance to occupation began as a largely secular nationalist movement and gradually morphed into one in which Islamists have taken the lead and secularists struggle to keep up. The same could happen in Iraq, in a telescoped time frame—and if it did, that would drastically change the strategic calculus for all participants, including those who want a federal, stable democratic state to emerge. Radical Islamists—even Iraqis—might deem an Iraq that is a quasi-permanent venue for jihad against the United States preferable to any peaceful outcome. Terrorists operating under this ideological framework will keep bombing, regardless of elections or good government.

To avoid this disaster scenario and marginalize those who would destroy the state regardless of consequences, the great challenge for an elected Iraqi government in which Shiʿis are the most numerous will be to assure Iraq's Sunnis that they will not be treated as they treated the Shiʿa and the Kurds. To draw again on the game theorists, the Shiʿa and the Kurds must convince the overwhelming majority of Sunnis that their interests will be better served in a democratic government in which power will alternate than by continuing the insurgency to the point of civil war. This is a complicated game, of course. One reason for the Sunni insurgency during the occupation was that Sunnis wanted to convince the Shiʿa and the Kurds that oppressing them or simply denying them a full share of state resources would be very costly. Certainly Shiʿis and Kurds who lost family members to the Sunni-dominated Baʿth regime (at least half a million dead, and 1.3 million missing according to the CPA) initially felt very unsympathetic to Sunni concerns for equal treatment. It will take time for the new majorities in Iraq to realize the necessity—for their own survival—of keeping Sunnis placated, and indeed of making them partners. Whether a violent insurgency will convince them of this, or of the opposite lesson, is an open question. It is one reason why the insurgency was always such a high-risk strategy for Sunnis.

In the real world, ideologies and emotions infuse and inflect the model of what "rational" behavior is supposed to produce. So the insurgents could draw on a deep well of old-fashioned anti-American sentiment, alongside justifiable fears of retaliation from some Shi'is and Kurds. The situation was also profoundly dynamic. The insurgents managed, at various points, to call down the considerable military might of the United States against them, as for example in Falluja in April 2004, when the killing and mutilation of four U.S. contractors led directly to an invasion of the city in which some six hundred Iraqis died. This retaliation inevitably alienated Sunnis who lost relatives in the fighting, whose homes were invaded by American soldiers, and who were subjected to daily search at checkpoints. Its failure led to the installation of an ex-Iraqi army general as head of a force tasked with restoring order in the city. Revenge may be "rational" as a deterrent strategy in some circumstances, but it can also get out of hand, and forward-looking game theory has trouble fully accounting for it. There is thus no guarantee that the Sunni Arabs of Iraq will accept any government that comes into being as a result of the American invasion, even if it is properly elected—and the possibility that this will precipitate a civil war remains the greatest single threat to the emergence of a legitimate, democratic Iraq, greater even than continuing jihadi terrorism coming primarily from without.

Yet ideology can work in both directions, fueling resistance and offering the possibility for reconciliation. Iraqi identity, however much it may be a product of colonial circumstance, remains a durable force. That identity is contested, not merely in the ordinary sense that all national identities are subject to debate and disagreement, but in the more profound way that national identities are in play when nation-states are undergoing traumatic reorganization. For many Sunnis, Iraqi identity long meant a state unconsciously identified with Sunni particularity, filtered through the lens of nationalist Baʿthism. Shiʿi Iraqis are now challenging this conception, at a minimum through their mere presence in active political roles, and also through public demonstrations at which the images displayed are of the martyrs ʿAli and Husayn, not Saddam. But it is important to note that Arab Iraqis, whether Sunni or Shiʿi, have not (yet) abandoned the project of defining an Iraqi identity. The wedge of Sunni on Shiʿi violence could conceivably change this over time, but during the occupation, at least, in the Shiʿi areas of southern Iraq, there was no significant support for independence from Baghdad, nor for the emergence of a homogeneous Shiʿi state. Indeed, one effect of the simultaneous Sunni and Shiʿi uprisings of April 2004 was to fuel a strand of Iraqi-unity rhetoric, with Shiʿis supporting Sunnis in Falluja, and Sunnis, for their part, exhibiting posters of Muqtada Sadr.

The point is that "artificial" national identities, products of the colonial era, have a surprising capacity to endure, at least in the Arab world. Indeed, it is almost astonishing to note that the specific national identities of Arab countries, almost all of them colonial products in one sense or another, today seem to have more weight than does the more general "Arab" identity associated with anticolonial Pan-Arabism. In other words, one reason to suspect that nation building may succeed in Iraq is that, at least outside of Kurdistan, an Iraqi identity already exists there. It is not as though primordial identities have reemerged or been reinvented, Balkan style, to destroy the artificial colonial state in Iraq. The Kurds, whose identity is nationality-seeking, do want autonomy, but they seem for the moment prepared to seek it within an Iraqi framework. In his bilingual speech at the signing of the TAL, Kurdish Democratic Party leader Massoud Barzani said that, because of the federal model contemplated by the interim law, for the first time he felt proud to be an Iraqi; and Arab Iraqis badly want the country to hold together.

Democracy, of course, is a much tougher nut to crack. The best case scenario would involve elected elites sharing power and distributing resources roughly in proportion to the relative numbers of different groups in the population, while respecting basic civil liberties. Iraq has been held together in the past only by a dominant single faction capable of keeping the loyalty of the army. During the occupation, the sole player in Iraq with even a fighting chance of preserving control was the United States, with its 140,000 troops. If U.S. troops were to leave precipitately, without being replaced by competent security forces from elsewhere, the state could disintegrate, just as it did in April 2003, after the fall of the old regime. The reason would be the extraordinary costs of coordination that must be overcome to produce a functioning state with the capacity to enforce its dictates and laws. One reason for the relative smoothness of the Eastern European transformations—the state collapse in Iraq makes those postcommunist transfers of power seem almost miraculously trouble-free—is that, with the exception of Yugoslavia, the states were not allowed to collapse. Once the state has gone, however, rebuilding it is a lengthy and costly process.

The strongest reason why, during the occupation period, power-sharing democracy still had a plausible chance of emerging in Iraq—despite the very great obstacles that I have described—was simply that no power association in the country could reasonably believe that it alone would be able to govern the country and dominate everybody else.[35] The Sunni Arabs were in the process of realizing that their days of dominion are done. In the long run, the only viable strategy for them is to reach some sort of reconciliation with those whom they previously oppressed. The phenomenon of Sunni dominance may have grown to seem natural to many Iraqis over three-quarters of a century, but it would not have come into being without the external intervention of the British, who built upon a power structure that was itself a relic of Ottoman control. Once the Sunnis had control of the state apparatus, the discovery of oil enabled a rentier arrangement in which foreign buyers funded their dominance by the purchase of oil. Now that the state has been taken from them, the Sunnis cannot get it back, whatever they may imagine.

Eventually, then, the insurgents ought to realize the long-term futility of resistance. Even an Islamically inspired broad-based Sunni insurgency—which did not emerge in Iraq during the occupation—must have *some* reasonable hope of success to garner broad popular support so long as it is bringing down privation on the Sunni population. The greatest short-term problem was how to create a Sunni leadership that could boast internal legitimacy but was not irretrievably tainted by Baʿthist ties. Without such a leadership, the insurgency stood to gain new life. Elections held out some hope of producing a leadership connected to the interests of ordinary Sunnis, though. Although electoral politics bring out divisive ideologies, Sunni leaders, once chosen, will have an incentive to serve their constituents' interests in returning to ordinary life—especially if the resistance comes to look like a dead end.

The Shiʿa, for their part, believed correctly through the occupation period that a system of electoral democracy would be to their advantage. But the Sunni insurgency slowly taught them that it would do no good to have an electoral majority if the opposition were disloyal, rather than loyal. As a consequence, their leadership had an incentive to extend a hand of forgiveness to any new Sunni leadership that may emerge. This could actually be easier for elected politicians who draw much of their support from the imprimatur of the Shiʿi clergy than it would be for politicians who relied exclusively on denominational or ethnic solidarity. Clergy can provide cover. The hard part, though, will be to create institutions that will give Sunnis a reasonable hope of garnering a fair share of the spoils of electoral victory. If all Shiʿa were to vote as one bloc, their 60 percent would win every national election and hold out no hope for the Sunnis. But one can predict with some confidence that ordinary politics will eventually take effect, and the Shiʿa will divide into multiple political parties that will, in the end, have to look for Sunni partners to create parliamentary majorities.

The Kurds, finally, never aspired to dominate the rest of the country but rather sought the protection of an Iraqi federation, which they need to survive in their rough neighborhood. They will thus be open, in the future, to forming alliances with Sunni and Shiʿa alike, because the fact that they are not Arabs means that, in the background, there always exists the possibility that Sunni Arabs and Iraqi Shiʿi Arabs might turn against them. Indeed, in internal Governing Council debates over the TAL, it was striking that the stronger Kurdish demands grew, the weaker the Shiʿa-Kurdish alliance became. Arab Iraqi identity was still strong; and resistance to the dismemberment of the country—by Americans or Kurds—was one of the handful of issues that could easily bridge the Sunni-Shiʿa divide. So long as the Kurds remain within Iraq, they will take friends wherever they can find them. That, indeed, has been their political history—with the important caveat that those friends have always been prepared to sell them out at a moment's notice.

What differentiates the federal, democratic, power-sharing solution from the one that the British undertook to structure is that where they set out to create a single dominant power—a Sunni monarchy that would be beholden to the British Empire which gave it life[36]—the United States and United Nations have sought to produce a state at least minimally acceptable to all the major interests in Iraqi society, in which the government would not be comparably beholden. Where the British imported a king from Arabia, the Coalition resisted, initially at least, the temptation to impose an exile government with little local legitimacy or visible support. If only in this sense, the U.S. nation-building project was not classically imperial: the eventual elected Iraqi government was meant to owe its legitimacy to local political forces, not to the imperial power.

Democracy, then, was not merely the best political arrangement that could work in contemporary Iraq. Once it was realized that no single player could create an effective tyranny, democracy was also the only option other than chaos. If the United States had cut a side deal with an Iraqi general prior to the war, and replaced Saddam with a less malevolent substitute, then perhaps Sunni domination could have continued. There were, at the time, voices within the U.S. government calling for exactly that solution—more realistic than the counterplan of an Iraqi exile imported from abroad, and even more cynical. But in any event, the United States did not choose that option, and this fateful decision guaranteed the impossibility of maintaining the old arrangements that the British put in place and Saddam refined through his own distinctive methods.

By saying that legitimate, democratic government in Iraq had a chance of emerging after the occupation, and may have a chance still, I do not mean to suggest a positive outcome was certain at any point. Far from it. The odds of success were low, and without a sustained U.S. commitment to preserving the peace, they may continue to drop, as they steadily did during the occupation year. But the alternative is also unacceptable. Removing security guarantees would mean allowing something that would closely approximate anarchy—a product, let me remind you, of our own choice to invade. Such a state would be much worse than Afghanistan as a breeding ground for terror—but far more important, it would spell disaster for the lives of ordinary Iraqis, tens of thousands of whom could die in riots or civil war. And it would sit on 10 percent of the world's proven oil reserves, within easy spilling-over distance of a further 30 percent elsewhere in the Gulf. There should be arguments enough here both for self-proclaimed realists and for people who care about the morality of our engagement in Iraq. A failed Iraq would threaten regional stability and would make the world less safe—but it would also be a humanitarian disaster almost entirely of U.S. making.

The consequences of premature withdrawal for the lives of Iraqis bring us to the question of the ethical structure of Wilsonian nation building, with its paternalistic rhetoric and neocolonial governance models. Even if our self-protective objectives for producing a legitimate democracy coincide with the interests of Iraqis, doesn't the legacy of the Wilsonian mandates reveal that the contradictions of nation building will overwhelm this coincidence of interests? Knowing what we do about colonialism and empire, how can we talk about taking on this kind of nation building today? The question is devastating and the challenge enormous. But it will have to wait for the next chapter.

CHAPTER TWO

Trusteeship, Paternalism, and Self-Interest

IN BAGHDAD DO WE LAY OUR SCENE. SPECIFICALLY, IN the auditorium of the Iraqi Lawyers Association, a pleasant modern meeting room in the Mansur neighborhood built to hold eight hundred, and on this day in mid-May 2003 filled to the brim with closer to a thousand Iraqi lawyers and other hangers-on. For a blessed half hour, the air-conditioning runs, and one is reminded that favored quasi-governmental institutions under the Baʿth regime actually fared rather well. The looting that devastated Baghdad and did perhaps $10 billion worth of damage in two weeks has left the Lawyers Association untouched except for a few broken windowpanes. Then the air-conditioning goes. The compressors are fine, the superintendent tells me, but power has just been cut to the whole neighborhood. The temperature begins to rise.

Today the second-highest-ranking U.S. official assigned to the Ministry of Justice in Iraq is meeting the Iraqi bar, or at least those lawyers in Baghdad who by word of mouth heard about the meeting. That official is Donald Campbell, a New Jersey Superior Court judge in civilian life, a major general in the Army Reserve, and an all-around decent man with no prior experience in the Middle East. Judge Campbell, as I always called him, is wearing a suit and tie, as are the great majority of older men in the room. The younger lawyers have left their ties at home. There are also perhaps a hundred women in the meeting, most in Western clothes, some wearing head scarves, and one wearing not only a full head covering but also an enveloping black *abayeh* and white cotton gloves.

The state of the room is one of barely controlled chaos. Judge Campbell is sitting on the dais to the left of Fatima, the Iraqi translator on whom he has come to rely. She is in her forties, not a lawyer, generous and patient. On the other side of Judge Campbell is the president of the Iraqi Lawyers Association. He's wearing a suit, too, slightly better cut than the regulation-issue Romanian article favored by rank-and-file former Baʿthists. The fuss is about him. From all over the hall, men are standing up and shouting in Arabic that the president is a Baʿthist. More than that, they are saying that he was Uday Hussein's personal attorney, and special counsel to the Iraqi Olympic Association, which in recent years had been Uday's fiefdom.

People are yelling at Judge Campbell, too, not that he can understand them. They are telling him that they are outraged at his sitting down beside such a criminal, and that they thought the United States came to rid them of the Baʿth. It is impossible to tell how many of the shouters are actually members of the Iraqi Lawyers Association, as opposed to outside agitators, but that is hardly the main point. After an hour or so, it is clear that they are not going to stop shouting. With Fatima translating, Judge Campbell has tried desperately to call the meeting to order. He has explained patiently that he would be glad to hear what they have to say if only they will take turns and speak one by one. It's not going to happen. This is a quasi-spontaneous protest action, which may have started by design of a few but is now gathering momentum. Judge Campbell has to make a decision.

During the shouting, I've been canvassing the room. I focus on lawyers my own age, and I ask everyone the same question: what is going on? The younger crowd is unanimous. The president is a crony of the old regime, and what is going on is that some in the audience will not let the meeting begin if he is on the dais. The people I am talking to, by necessity standing toward the periphery of the room, don't really seem to have a strong view about whether the protest is right or wrong. They would like to get on with the meeting, at which they expect to hear about the status of the courts and, more to the point, their salaries and job prospects in post-Saddam Iraq. But no one that I encounter denies that the president of the Lawyers Association was closely tied to Uday. It seems to have been a fact universally acknowledged.

I make my way up onto the dais to confer with Judge Campbell. "What do you think?" he asks me. "Well, Judge," I say, "I think you've got two options. We can leave or you can fire the president." The judge nods, and I see that he's about to make a decision. I walk to the side of the stage. The judge turns to Fatima to make sure that she's ready; then he addresses the crowd. "Many of you are telling me that this man, your president, is a Ba'thist. It is the policy of the Coalition Provisional Authority not to work with the Ba'th Party. Sir, you are no longer the president of the Iraqi Lawyers Association. Please step down from the stage." By the time the translation is finished, the applause is deafening.

But our little regime change is not yet over. The president has something to say, and Judge Campbell tries to silence the crowd so he can say it. "You have no right to do this," protests the president. "The mechanism for election of the president of the Lawyers Association is specified in the Iraqi Lawyers Law. You have no authority to remove me from office." There is muttering from the crowd, especially those who remained largely silent during the shouting before. "He's right, of course," I hear one of the young lawyers saying beside me. "There is such a law." Judge Campbell beckons me over again. I've led the judge into a legal pickle. "Now what?" he asks.

I've got an answer, but I am not sure the crowd is going to like it. "Judge, I recommend you tell him that under the international law of occupation, the CPA is authorized to take all measures to restore public life and order, and that pursuant to the authority vested in you by Ambassador Bremer, you have removed him." The judge is back at the microphone. He's about to make a legal argument in front of a thousand Iraqi lawyers, so it had better be good. "Pursuant to international law we are empowered to restore public life and order. De-Ba'thification is the order of Ambassador Bremer. Sir, you are removed. Please stand down."

Then it happens. The president picks up his papers; leaves the dais; leaves the room. The crowd calms down. Judge Campbell calls the meeting to order, and it starts like every other meeting you've ever been to, with a queue and a time limit for speaking. The Iraqi Lawyers Association considers its options, and several members recommend another meeting later in the week to elect an interim, acting board to replace the president and oversee national elections for a new president. It's over. International law has done its work.

But what work was that? By citing Article 43 of the Annex to the Hague Convention of 1907, which requires the occupying power to "take all the measures in his power to restore *l'ordre et la vie publics*, while respecting, unless absolutely prevented, the laws in force in the country,"[1] Judge Campbell had proffered a legal justification for superseding the Iraqi Lawyers Law. As I discovered over the next few hours, recanvassing the room, some lawyers there were indeed willing to accept that the firing occurred pursuant to our legal authority. Others, though, pointed out correctly that Iraqi law remains in place under conditions of occupation.[2] They vociferously insisted that the Iraqi Lawyers Law was valid law, and that while they were glad to see the president go, they were convinced we had accomplished that outcome illegally. To them this was just a show of force.

Who was right? It is impossible to deny that, if we were not in a country under military occupation, the president would never have walked away. Although there were just two or three soldiers in the auditorium when the dismissal took place, the president stood down because, in the end, we had the guns. Seen in this light, international law was nothing more than a fig leaf for an act of naked power. Indeed, suppose that our hastily formulated legal interpretation was not the best reading of the Hague regulation: what would happen? Basically, nothing. Like most provisions of the law of occupation, including the Geneva Conventions, the Hague laws do not provide for their own enforcement by any court or other judicial body. Since the Coalition would decide for itself whether it had violated international law, it seems plausible to conclude that what transpired in the auditorium was not law but force.

From a subtly different perspective, however, something did happen in that room full of lawyers when Judge Campbell articulated a specifically legal answer to a specifically legal challenge leveled by the outgoing president. The president would not have claimed that we lacked the authority to fire him unless he thought it would have some impact either on the audience or on us—more probably the former than the latter, since the entire invasion had been doubtful as a matter of international law. The president wanted to undercut the legitimacy of his removal in the eyes of the assembled lawyers of Baghdad. By invoking the law of occupation, we were trying to reestablish the legitimacy of that removal. We wanted that in-the-field, wholly unplanned decision to appear more than arbitrary, to fit into a defensible paradigm in which we deployed coercion *for a reason*. The reason was provided by the international legal convention. We were exercising the power to fire the president of the Iraqi Lawyers Association in order to promote the interests of Iraqis in public order and public life.

The reason we were offering, then, may have been legal in the sense that it was derived from a convention to which the United States—and for that matter, Iraq—had bound itself as a signatory; but it was, more important, an *ethical* reason we were providing for our high-handed behavior. As lawyers speaking to other lawyers, we were relying on the shorthand of textual provisions that could be looked at and debated by jurists of reason. As occupiers, though—and make no mistake, that is what we were—we were trying to tell the Iraqis in the room that we were circumventing the Iraqi Lawyers Law in order to serve their interests in being free of the Baʿth regime and, more immediately, in getting started with the meeting that would discuss the future of the association and, by extension, the future of the country. The ethical dimension of this argument depended upon the implicit claim that we were breaking the Iraqis' law *for their own good.*

It is hard to write these words now—much harder, in fact, than it would have been to make the argument explicit in Baghdad, where it seemed plainly obvious in May 2003 that whatever the uncertainty of the situation, Judge Donald Campbell was infinitely preferable to Uday's consigliere. The reasons it is difficult to express the sentiment that we were trying to exercise the occupier's authority for the benefit of the Iraqis present are two: first, it sounds horribly paternalistic; second, it sounds as if it might be a lie. In this chapter, I will examine both of those forms of skeptical reaction, each of which can be read as growing from the actual experiences of colonialism, especially the quasi-colonialism associated with the mandates created by the League of Nations in the wake of World War I. Before I do, though, I want first to lay out the ethical vision that these twin skepticisms call into question. The best, most honest name for the vision of occupation and nation building that I have in mind is *trusteeship.*

The idea of trusteeship has a rich, varied, and complex history in international law and theory. It is sometimes traced to the Spanish canonists Bartolomé de Las Casas and Francisco de Vitoria, the latter of whom argued that the Indians of the New World, possessed of polities, laws, and even religion, were reasonable men entitled in principle to rule themselves, and on whose behalf "wardship" could be exercised by Europeans until they could self-govern.[3] Trusteeship continued to figure subsequently in the ideology of empire. In a famous speech in the parliamentary debate about the powers of the East India Company in 1783, Edmund Burke argued that political power exercised over others—in this case, old-world Indians— should be understood as a trust for the benefit of the ruled.[4] As may also fairly be said of Vitoria's view, Burke's position simultaneously authorized colonial domination and constrained it from being exercised without regard to the colonial subjects. Depending on one's perspective, this argumentative move was either a brilliant piece of enlightened thinking or a devilish trick to cover the injustice of colonialism. I think it is probably closest to the truth to say it was a bit of both.

I shall return to Burke's conception of trusteeship a bit later in this chapter; but for the moment, I want to draw your attention to the place of the idea of trusteeship specifically in the international law of occupation, which is somewhat distinct from its place in colonial theory more generally. In retrospect, it was no coincidence that the provision of international law I suggested to Judge Campbell came not from the Fourth Geneva Convention, crafted in the humanitarian ideological environment of the late 1940s, but from the earlier Hague regulations, produced before World War I. The Hague regulations embody a theory of occupation according to which the country doing the occupying (the "occupant," in the relevant legal jargon, although I shall consistently use the more colloquial term "occupier") holds the population and land on behalf of its rightful, initial sovereign ruler, to whom it will be returned on cessation of hostilities.[5] In this model of trusteeship, the trustee is the occupier, and the beneficiary of the trust is the rightful sovereign, on whose behalf the occupier is holding the country. The people who live in the occupied country are themselves the thing being held in trust.

According to the Hague theory of trusteeship, the occupier-trustee is to do as little as possible to change the situation in the country it is holding in trust. Private property is to remain inviolate.

Pillage is forbidden. Tax collection "for the benefit of the state" is permitted, but only according to the rules in place before the occupation. The prior laws stay in place, subject only to the duty of the occupier to restore public life and order. Resources are to be treated as usufruct only, and are not to be exploited or expropriated.[6] Decisions taken pursuant to this authority are meant to be *restorative*, returning the population to the ordered state it is assumed to have been in prior to war. Such decisions are not unlike the investment decisions a trustee might make in the exercise of his power over a trust: if the market conditions change, the trustee might have to sell or buy accordingly. The population may get something out of this arrangement, but once again, the ultimate assumed beneficiary is the displaced sovereign who will regain control after a treaty is reached.

The ideology of trusteeship changed, though, under the influence of Wilsonian ideals of democratic self-determination. The mandate system that came into being with the League of Nations conceptualized the power receiving the mandate—in practice, Great Britain or France—as charged with developing the political situation of the country in question to the point where it would satisfy the characteristics necessary for assuming its own sovereignty. Sovereign nations-in-waiting were understood to exist who were "not yet able to stand by themselves under the strenuous conditions of the modern world."[7] What these nations needed was "development," and that development must be facilitated from without.

The concept of trusteeship described the relationship between the rest of the world and these undeveloped peoples:

> There should be applied the principle that the well-being and development of such peoples form a sacred trust of civilization and that securities for the formance of this trust should be embodied in this Covenant.[8]

The metaphor of trusteeship did not stop there. The principle of this "sacred trust" would be implemented by "advanced nations" to whom "the tutelage of such peoples should be entrusted."[9]

The nominal trust relationship under the mandate system, then, was to be double-barreled. The thing held in trust was the well-being and development of undeveloped peoples. It was up to all of "civilization" to act as trustees; and the Covenant of the League of Nations was itself to be the trust document that would guarantee and provide "securities" for the trust to come into being. Then the signatories to the Covenant would further delegate—or "entrust," as the Covenant had it—to the advanced nations the responsibility to deliver well-being and development. Subject to the supervision of the League, the advanced nations would act as trustees, making the relevant decisions that would guide the nascent nations toward self-determination.

The paternalism of this formulation could not have been more explicit; and nowhere in the world that it characterized as undeveloped and in need of tutelage did it sit well with those who knew of it. Moreover, as I shall have occasion to discuss a bit later, the great powers made free to distort the trust relationship and to serve no one's interests but their own. To an important degree, the theory of the mandates brought together elements of the kind of trusteeship associated with the law of occupation—the mandates were, after all, territory conquered from the Ottoman Empire—with the trusteeship long associated with colonialism and connected to the vague idea of benefiting the natives. Then the mandatory theory infused this admixture with the modern notion of national self-determination.

Our contemporary conceptions of nation building are still plagued by this legacy: the classical formulation of the goals of nation building is grounded in a vision of trusteeship that was both ethically troubling and practically flawed. These concerns led to a gradual decline in the appeal of trusteeship in the latter half of the twentieth century. The United Nations created a Trusteeship Council, but the trusts it administered were all extinguished over the next quarter century as the ideology of decolonization made them seem obsolete. The Trusteeship Council ceased to operate in 1994 with the termination of the trusteeship of Palau. Although the UN-led transitional administrations in Bosnia, Kosovo, and East Timor have given rise to renewed discussion of the idea of trusteeship in the international context, none of the formal Security Council resolutions associated with those administrations embraced the concept.[10]

In Iraq, however, the concept of trusteeship reemerged for an intriguing (some would say telling) reason: in the absence of an internationally authorized transitional administration, the Coalition Provisional Authority was, juridically speaking, an occupier. The Security Council resolution recognizing that fact called on the CPA to adhere to the Hague Regulations and Geneva Conventions.[11] As Eyal Benvenisti has noted, this represented the first time in some years that occupier status was declared by the international community and acknowledged by the occupier.[12] The law of occupation was back in business in Iraq—and the idea of trusteeship returned with it, in one of its forms.

In the light of the history of the idea of trusteeship, which I have given here in a very truncated form, you may well approach the very term with grave doubts. I know that I do. Nonetheless, I want to ask you to consider yet another formulation of the doctrine of trusteeship in nation building: one that takes seriously the question of exactly what is being held in trust, by whom, and for whose benefit.

The approach I want to suggest differs from its predecessors in that it takes trusteeship not as a vague metaphor but as the starting point for a hardheaded analysis of the exercise of decision-making authority, one drawn from contemporary economic thinking in the theory of agents and principals.[13] This simplified model of the trust involves three parties: the one who creates the trust (again, to use jargon, the "settlor"), the trustee, and the beneficiary. By hypothesis, the settlor takes some property within his own authority and confers control of it on the trustee to use it for the good of the beneficiary.

Applying trusteeship analysis to nation building is tricky business. Consider the difficult question of defining the thing held in trust. In the Hague model, it was the occupied population and the land. This view seems entirely unsatisfactory in terms of our own contemporary political theory, because it assumes that people and land belong to the government that rules over them, and that they are objects of governance rather than subjects. The League of Nations mandatory model maintained that a people's well-being and development were the things held in trust. This seems slightly more attractive, because it aspires to eventual self-government—but in the final analysis, the idea that my "development" from one stage to another can be put in the hands of some third party does not seem ethically sustainable from the standpoint of autonomy.

There is another possibility, however: the thing held in trust under conditions of occupation and nation building may simply be the authority to govern. This approach derives from a standard way of thinking about agency and ordinary democratic government. In a representative democracy, citizens do not rule themselves directly. Outside of a New England town meeting or the idealized Athenian constitution, the citizens themselves do not vote on every issue. Instead, we delegate governmental decision making in the realms of legislation, execution, and administration alike. This form of delegation can be characterized as the conferral of authority to a trustee to exercise power on one's behalf. Here Burke once again becomes relevant. He may have spoken of trusteeship in the context of emergent colonial rule, but he believed in trusteeship as the requisite condition for all political authority, including domestic and

representative power: "[A]ll political power which is set over men,"
he held, "ought to be some way or other exercised ultimately for
their benefit."[14] In speaking to his own constituents in 1774, Burke
asserted that "[y]our representative owes you, not his industry only,
but his judgment; and he betrays, instead of serving you, if he sacri-
fices it to your opinion."[15] Although Burke's view is itself controversial, and subject to the charge of paternalism, it may nonetheless
be defended as a reasonable way to give effect to the structure of
electoral democracy, in which representatives do not submit every
issue to their constituents but instead stand for office on regular
occasions. There is, in other words, nothing inherently oppressive
about the idea of trusteeship applied to the authority to govern: it
is endemic to representative democracy itself.

This model of trusteeship has a great deal in common with the
problems that arise any time one person delegates to another person the responsibility to act as an agent on her behalf. The scope
of the agent's authority to act in the interests of the principal must
be determined, and the principal must calculate the best way to
ensure that her interests are actually promoted. The cost of moni-
toring the agent and the costs associated with those situations in
which the agent does not act in the principal's interests are both
included in the category that economists call "the costs of agency."

We sometimes use the heuristic device of thinking about the
costs of agency to consider problems arising in ordinary representative democracy: according to this view, our elected representatives
are our agents, and we must both devise some scheme for supervising them and determine the costs of what happens when they act
in their own interests, rather than ours.[16] If we can think of the
elected government as our agent, then we can also imagine the
arrangement in which government holds in trust the authority to
govern us. We give that responsibility to our elected officials for a
limited time, it is true—but trusts can be limited in time as well. Our
officials govern us according to laws, of course—but the trustee's

authority is also exercised according to rules. The government is elected to govern according to our interests, in much the same sense that the trustee administers the trust on behalf of the beneficiary.

If the authority to govern can be thought of as a trust, then in a democracy, it is clear in principle who gives it to whom: we, the electorate, give it to our chosen officials. The people themselves are both settlor and beneficiary. But who gives the occupier authority to govern under conditions of nation building? At the most literal level, it clearly is not the occupied population, who ordinarily will not have chosen to be occupied, or at least will not have voted for it. It sounds preposterous as a realistic matter to expect the occupier to hold a referendum the day the old government falls, asking if it may be authorized to rule in turn. So the analogy to a trustee who has been expressly authorized to exercise authority over the thing placed in trust cannot succeed. Yet at the same time, it is also true that *somebody* must govern in the aftermath of the fall of an old regime. The only realistic option is for the occupier to take the reins of government. The model of trusteeship does not legitimate the fact that it is the occupier who will be governing; but it can shed light on the responsibilities that the occupier-as-government will then have toward the country to be governed.

Put simply, the occupying force owes the same ethical duties to the people being governed that an ordinary, elected democratic government would owe them. It must govern in their interests; and it must not put its own narrow interests ahead of the interests of the people being governed. When we see government putting itself first, we call it unethical. Of course, we accept that elected representatives have interests of their own—chiefly the goal of being re-elected[17]—just as, I have argued, it is permissible for the nation builder to form goals on the basis of its interests. (Indeed, even ordinary trustees get compensated for their labor and are not presumed to act purely out of altruism.) But the reason we consider the elected representative's goal formation defensible is that it presumably coincides with the voters' interests. Similarly, the nation builder may pursue its own interests in security so long as these coincide with the interests of the occupied people.

There is an ever green debate about whether elected representatives ought to do in office what the majority of the people want them to do in a given moment, or what, in their best judgment, they believe would be best for the people as a whole.[18] But both positions in this debate, as well as the reasonable compromises between them, agree that elected representatives owe it to the people to act on their behalf, depending on how that is defined. Agent-principal theories of representative government similarly assume that the people, acting as principals, aim to get government to do what they want; and such approaches often implicitly introduce the normative assumption that this aspiration is the right one.

Beyond the question of how the government comes into being, there is a further, glaring difference between the electorate and an occupied people. The electorate gets to declare its verdict on the government in power by voting in the next elections. This is one of the main ways in which the principal keeps control of its agents; and it is missing from the context of occupation and nation building. L. Paul Bremer was never going to stand for office in Iraq, even if many of the Iraqis who worked with him will eventually have to do just that. This difference raises a further challenge to the trusteeship model I am proposing: who guards the guardians? Who keeps an eye on the trustee to make sure that the people's interests are served, and not exclusively the trustee's?[19]

Under the Hague model, the rightful sovereign was probably expected to keep a distant, watchful eye on how his occupied territory was being governed. Even if we had no objection to the anti-democratic dynamics of this model, it will not work under conditions of nation building, where we hope to have said good riddance to the old government. The Covenant of the League of Nations was structured so that the League would have the responsibility of keeping an eye on the countries administering the mandates. The British in Iraq spent a good deal of time privately worrying that the League would think they were doing a less than creditable job of encouraging Iraq's political development.[20] Yet the problem is that the League—or the "international community," to use the current shorthand—may not care deeply about the people under occupation, or if the international community does care, it may lack the means to influence a determined occupier.

The law of trusts, however, is realistic about who has the greatest interest in enforcing the terms of the trust: the beneficiary herself, who is authorized to come into court and challenge the trustee's management.[21] I have just said that the occupied people themselves will not ordinarily get the chance to vote on the occupying power during the period of occupation, so that option for protesting the management of their government is excluded. But a wide range of other options remains—and it must be the ethical duty of the occupier-government to make sure that these avenues of review and supervision remain open and effective.

The most obvious of these mechanisms are the freedoms of speech and assembly. The occupied people must have the capacity to speak out loudly when they believe that their government is being mismanaged. They must be able to do so through the media, but they must also be able to protest by taking to the streets, so long as they do so peacefully, in order to draw the occupier's attention to the intensity of their objections and the magnitude of support that these objections enjoy. Speech and assembly, after all, are the main means used by people living in an ordinary democracy to supervise their government between elections. The occupier will be tempted to limit criticism of itself and the right to protest or march;[22] but these temptations must be resisted, not so much because speech and assembly are fundamental rights—though they surely are—but because these are the most effective means for drawing the occupier's attention (and the world's, for that matter) to what the occupier is doing wrong.

There are other means of supervision, as well—but these ultimately must come from the occupier's committing itself to working with some representatives of the occupied people. This relationship can be treacherous for both sides and for the occupied people as a whole. But there is no ethical substitute for the occupation government's undertaking to engage with citizens of the occupied country who will be able to play, among other things, the role of supervision.

A range of relationships may be undertaken. The one least tainted by charges of "collaboration" arises when the occupying authority takes upon itself to weigh heavily the input of particular leaders who seem capable of commanding popular support. Ayatollah Sistani played this role in occupied Iraq. He functioned as the democratic (or at least the majoritarian) conscience of the occupation, reminding the Coalition that it had declared its intention to deliver democracy; that democracy inevitably must include elections at some point; and that in elections, the majority should prevail. At the other end of the continuum, there are the citizens of the occupied country who exercise power formally delegated to them by the occupation government. Transitional ministers fill this bill. Their job, ethically speaking, is not only to exercise their technocratic functions, but to ensure that the occupier is called to account internally if it seems to be slighting the interests of the occupied people in favor of its own.

In between these extremes are the selected-but-unelected members of councils, whether they be municipal, regional, or national, as was the Iraqi Governing Council. Such bodies have a responsibility to represent the interests of the citizens. Because they are made up of politicians who aspire to be elected in the future, they have the right incentives to do what they think the people would like them to do. (Of course, they also have the incentive to become first-movers who will try to gain more than their fair share of political power in the country; but if there are to be free elections, it will be hard for them to do this without actually satisfying their potential constituents' needs.) It is the corresponding responsibility of the occupation government to take seriously the views expressed by these unelected representatives, especially when those relate to divergences between the interests of the occupier and those of the occupied.

To sum up, then, the version of trusteeship that I want to propose restricts the trustee to governing in the manner in which an ordinary, democratically elected government would. This approach emphasizes not the broad powers of the trustee to bring the occupied nation into being—the emphasis under the Wilsonian version—but rather the primacy of the beneficiaries of the trust, namely, the people being governed. The beneficiaries are best placed to supervise the exercise of the powers of the trust, just as an ordinary citizenry is best placed to keep its eye on the exercise of government. They must do so through public speech, assembly, and participation in the administration of government; and it is the ethical duty of the trustee to allow, and even to facilitate, these forms of participation. The model of the trust serves to underscore the fundamental, underlying duty that falls upon the occupation authority: it is exercising the power of government, and in this capacity it must put the interests of the governed ahead of its own.

Now that I have laid out what I believe to be a potentially attractive version of the trusteeship model, let me turn to the major objections to it. As I suggested earlier, the two most basic objections are the ethical and the practical. Ethically, trusteeship seems paternalistic and by definition heteronomous. Practically, experience suggests that trustees often act in their own interests, not those of the supposed beneficiaries of their actions. Abuses happen, both at the

individual level and, more broadly, at the national level. The outra-
geous abuse of prisoners in the military prison at Abu Ghraib was
certainly an instance of the former, and possibly of the latter as well.
Colonialism and occupation have, by their fruits, given trusteeship
a bad name.

Let us begin with the ethical objection, which on its face carries
tremendous weight. How can one seriously maintain, in the
twenty-first century, that the United States or its allies may justifiably take in their hands the government of other nations, with the
stated aspiration—you will recall from the first chapter—of establishing stable, democratically legitimate government? Who are we
to govern on behalf of others?

The ethical challenge is deepened when one considers the dozens
of failed nation-building exercises around the world, legacies of both
Wilsonianism and the differently oriented nation building of the
Cold War. The high failure rate strongly supports the basic intuition
that we do not know what we are doing—and one of the crucial
elements of any argument for autonomy is that people tend to
know themselves, better than others, how they ought best to live
their lives. On this view, one of the reasons why the Wilsonian
mandates and so many other nation-building exercises failed was
precisely that they embodied the ethically unattractive idea that advanced, knowledgeable, Western, and almost without exception
white people knew best how to shape the political development of
people who were undeveloped, Southern or Eastern, and almost
without exception nonwhite. It is not merely that the West does
not know better than the rest; it is that one of the West's cardinal
errors is thinking that it does know better.

Put another way, if our true goal is to produce the autonomy
associated with self-determination, it seems very odd to get there
by taking the powers of self-determination away from the people
under tutelage. The metaphor of children receiving an education
and eventually developing the wisdom and experience necessary

to enter the world of adulthood captures what is wrong with this approach. After all, as civilizations or as peoples, the rich West is certainly no older than those it subjects to nation building. It is tough to argue that it is collectively wiser. All that can reasonably be said is that, at present, the United States is richer and more powerful; and in the cases of Germany and Japan, even that was not true by much of a margin when war broke out.

Let me be very clear about what I wish to say next. To nation build successfully and ethically, we need to *abandon* the paternalistic idea that we know how to produce a functioning, successful democracy better than do others. This change in thinking is an extremely tall order, one that we by no means accomplished collectively or individually in Iraq. The paternalistic impulse runs deep in the project of nation building; one might even wonder whether we would be able to motivate ourselves to go on building in its absence.

One can begin, as I did, in the role of constitutional adviser, reminding oneself every morning not to end up drafting a constitution for others that ultimately has no chance of success or even of meaningful implementation. But even with good intentions, the background pressures are there. Western reporters regularly asked me when I would be done drafting the constitution of Iraq. I refrained from producing a document that would actually be the constitution; my job in the CPA was to advise Ambassador Bremer on constitutional affairs and to delineate some possible constitutional options and outcomes. Then, once I was outside government, I was fortunate enough to work directly with some of the Iraqis who were deeply involved in preliminary constitutional processes, including the drafting of the Transitional Administrative Law, which was intended to function as an interim constitution. Constitution writing, to succeed, must be done by Iraqis sensitive to their own politics, circumstances, and conditions. All that anyone else can do is give advice, and it is right and appropriate that, often, that advice will be rejected. When that happens, one's instinct is to advise that some particular constitutional arrangement has worked well in one place or another, and ought to be adopted despite Iraqis' objections. What I mean to say is that the cultural script of colonialism is easy to perform. Giving up the script is no easy task.

But give it up we must. By this I do *not* mean to argue that the project of nation building must be abandoned wholesale. I do not accept the view that the tension between democratic self-rule and the occupier's heteronomous authority amounts to an inherent ethical contradiction that cannot be satisfactorily addressed. I do believe, however, that the only way to nation build successfully is to recognize that there is nothing in our comparative advantages of wealth and power that gives us any special ability to identify the institutional structures that will succeed in producing democracy in a particular place. The best political scientists, constitutional theorists, and area experts are regularly wrong—largely because the combination of general expertise and knowledge of the local facts is so rare—and when the divergent views of a range of scholars are amalgamated, they may be even more wrong than any one of them would be in isolation.[23] Local Iraqis, or indeed citizens of any country undergoing nation building, of course also make mistakes. Romanticizing the infallible wisdom of local knowledge is just as egregious an error as assuming that our social science has all the answers. The right approach begins with the realization of the enormous uncertainty that permeates all areas of our predictive judgments about nation building.

So the reality is that we do not really know how to build a nation any better than do its citizens. Yet at the same time, there are circumstances in which a country badly needs external involvement if it is to have any hope of developing a democratically legitimate government. The classic situation, in contemporary terms, is one in which an autocratic government has collapsed, civil society has been weakened to the point of disappearance, and a range of different factions are trying to coalesce in the political vacuum. Typically, when these other conditions obtain, either the threat or the reality of violence looms in the background. Iraq after Saddam's fall was like this, but so, in a different sense, was the former Yugoslavia.[24]

These conditions, needless to say, are not propitious for the emergence of a stable and successful democracy. They are, rather, precisely the conditions under which it is difficult for representative political leadership to identify a common interest in power sharing and power alternation, and even more difficult to institutionalize those common interests. If conditions were promising, there would be little need for external nation building—the emergent democracies could make it on their own, as for example in postcommunist Poland. There civil society had slowly and painfully reconstituted itself under late communism, and elites both new and old understood that the consequence of an internal clash would be disastrous for all. With the removal of the Soviet Union as the interventive threat backing the government, the transition to democracy could occur.[25] In the countries I have in mind—Bosnia, Kosovo, Somalia, Iraq, Afghanistan, and others—there is precious little hope of success even with external nation building; but there is no hope at all for success without it.

The role of the nonpaternalistic nation builder is, in the first instance, to impose security by constituting a power large enough to prevent civil war or anarchy, and strong enough to enforce its will throughout the country. The importance of this job cannot be emphasized enough. All other aspects of nation building flow from it, and if it falters or fails, the nation-building project will certainly fail, too. The potential for internal unrest after the collapse of autocratic government is great anywhere, but it is especially likely where that government has prevented the emergence of a civil society that to some reasonable degree transcends citizens' other forms of identity. The reason this is important is that, the moment government collapses, people look first for existing power associations to help protect them.

Civil society can hold out the promise of protection through its deployment of reasoned discourse. The term is notoriously slippery; but by "civil society" I mean to identify nonstate organizations, not excluding political parties or religious groups, who set out to achieve various goals through coordinated, nonviolent action and advocacy.[26] Although civil society carries no guns, its existence depends upon a social agreement, reached through a combination of belief in the power of words and mutually reinforcing self-interest, which reduces the need for violence to resolve the problems of complex transitions. If this sounds naive or unworldly, recall that, outside of Yugoslavia and Romania, the transitions in the former Soviet bloc occurred essentially without violence—and these were not military takeovers.[27] The transitions depended upon language, used experimentally and ultimately effectively, deployed by people who acted in and through civil society associations. The possibility of violence was in the background, as it always is in human affairs— but it was civil society, more than any other force, that kept violence *in* the background.

If civil society does not exist, however—if there are simply no effective nonstate organizations doing useful things nonviolently— then people who are faced with the collapse of the autocratic government will deal with their justifiable fear of what happens next by looking to form new associations to protect them. They will want those organizations to have power, preferably of the military variety. They will often ally themselves in various forms of ethnic, familial, or denominational solidarity—and so militias will emerge. The role of identity must be treated delicately here. There is a tendency to assume or believe that people revert to primordial identities once the yoke of autocratic government is thrown off. You might call this the "ancient hatreds" theory, frequently used in popular literature to explain the collapse of Yugoslavia.[28]

In my view, the idea of reversion to old identity misses much of what is going on when new alliances form along apparently old lines in the aftermath of state collapse. In fact, people are looking to protect themselves, as you or I would under conditions of potential anarchy. They are quite literally seeking to create mutual protection associations not so different from those imagined by Robert Nozick in his early thought experiment, *Anarchy, State, and Utopia*.[29] Forming such mutual protection associations requires overcoming the costs of collective action—quite literally, figuring out who will be willing to join and can be trusted to pull his weight. Time is of the essence. The skies are darkening, and everyone else is running around trying to form mutual protection associations, too.

Under these conditions, any prior social bond may be useful in forming one's own mutual protection association faster and better than others. The more comprehensive the bond, the better, because it raises the likelihood that more people will join the association. In a perfect demonstration of a positive network externality, the greater the likelihood that more people will join the association, the greater the likelihood that people will identify that fact as a reason to join the association. It follows that, with the pressure on, individuals will take advantage of whatever markers of identity they already had—the bigger the better—to form mutual protection associations.[30]

Here the ideology of identity comes into play. After all, people are being called upon to make a crucial, possibly life-or-death decision about whom they will join. They will want, reasonably enough, to join an association whose members will feel the highest possible degree of loyalty and attachment. Brand-new identities are a bad bet, because it is hard to know in advance how much loyalty they will generate. That leaves so-called "traditional" identities, which may be local, familial, ethnic, or denominational. Among these, and leaving room for overlap, the citizens of a failed state will search for options. To the outside observer, it will look as though traditional identities have reemerged after years of latency. In a limited degree, in the sense I have explained, this will be true. But it will also appear to the outside observer that these old identities are arrayed against one another. From this state of affairs—also accurate, in a sense—he will conclude that he is in the presence of "ancient hatreds."

But this conclusion will be wrong. The reason adherents of the new-old identity groups are eyeing one another warily is that they have turned to these identities to form mutual protection associations. Identity was simply the shortest and best route to self-protection. In the absence of an external power capable of maintaining the balance, these protection associations may end up in a civil war. The reason will not be that they have always hated one another, although the ideology of identity being what it is, it is not impossible that they will begin to tell themselves that this is true. The reason they have a chance of killing each other is that the uncertainty of who will dominate whom is so high. The possibility of reconciliation and common entrance into a newly constituted democratic state remains; but that, too, requires overcoming the very high costs of coordination—and that will be the next task of the nation builder.

I intend to turn to that next step shortly. But before I do, let me make the foregoing account of the emergence of identity-based mutual protection associations more concrete using the example of Iraq. It has become commonplace to say that Saddam destroyed civil society, so let me provide an example of what that meant in practice, one drawn from our old friends at the Iraqi Lawyers Association. In the weeks following that energized meeting at which the president was removed, I returned to the Lawyers Association several times for meetings of various sizes, ranging from the eight hundred who turned out to vote for a slate of temporary directors, to the five men—all men, although several women were nominated—who won those elections. These meetings were fascinating, in a frustrating sort of way, because they showed me just how little I really understood the thought world of the Iraqis with whom I had the greatest amount in common.*

In one meeting, I was having an informal discussion with perhaps fifteen lawyers in their thirties and early forties about judicial corruption, a topic much on their minds. They took the view that perhaps 80 percent of Iraqi judges (there was some debate about the best estimate) were on the take. Their proposed solution was to set up a meeting with me at which they would give me the names of all the corrupt Iraqi judges. Since there were only a few hundred judges in the country, the numerical aspect of this proposal is perhaps less surprising than it initially sounds. But, obviously, the idiosyncratic list of a self-selected group of young lawyers would be of limited value.

"Look," I told them, "why don't you form a special committee on judicial corruption under the auspices of the Iraqi Lawyers Association. I have the feeling the new directors being elected right now would be excited by the idea. If you can speak with one voice, and produce a report that is endorsed or at least not rejected by the entire Lawyers Association, you're going to have a major impact on the problem of judicial corruption, because there is

---

* One chastening indication was my conversation with the only fully covered woman lawyer whom I met at the Lawyers Association, whose piety extended to a pair of cotton gloves that she wore indoors. She had volunteered to help coordinate and supervise the ballot counting, a key public role in convincing the lawyers that their votes were really going to mean something. She was the one who explained to me that I must hold up the ballot boxes and show them empty to the crowd immediately before the voting began, because previous practice had apparently been to fix the outcome by stuffing the boxes before the voting. In a quiet moment during the interminable, public vote counting (I found myself transported back to Palm Beach County, where I'd done a turn as a Gore litigator—except that the Iraqi vote counters were more efficient and more principled), she asked me whether I was married and had kids. When I told her that my wife and I had no offspring yet, she encouraged us to have some soon, since children were a blessing. Naturally enough, I asked her how many she had. She looked at me with astonishment bordering on contempt: "I would never marry a man," she said with an expression of slight superiority. "I am in love with my work." Score one for transnational first-wave feminism!

no other group in the country dealing with the issue. The CPA and eventually the Iraqi government will have to consider your recommendations."

By the end of this spontaneous little speech, I had lost my audience completely. To them, there was just one way to get things done: find the right man with power—which they mistakenly assumed to be me—and have him whisper in the ear of the right man above him. In a totalitarian dictatorship, I have no doubt, they would have been correct. (Perhaps you will say they were not unjustified in thinking that the CPA under Ambassador Bremer might be no different; in fact, though, any time any Iraqis acted collectively in the early phases of the occupation, the CPA snapped to attention and responded, if nothing else out of the hope to find civil society being born anywhere in Iraq.) I was witnessing what the absence of civil society looks like: no one trusts the value of collective public discourse to get anything done. The Iraqi Lawyers Association was not a site of civil society. It was the empty shell of civil society. The auditorium and the offices had survived regime change, but there was no one home.

In an environment like this, ordinary Iraqis had no one to speak for them about the need to avoid lawlessness and violence. The fact that no leader could really do anything to stop the looting—which lasted until everything of value had been taken, and not a moment less—was the first piece of evidence that all bets were off. That, and not simply the extraordinary economic costs, was the true tragedy of the immediate postwar period. Iraqis got the message that the United States was not in charge, and that no one else was, either. In the second week of May, I was chatting with the local folks in a poor Shi'i neighborhood of Baghdad. After some questions about electricity and the schools—to which, of course, there were no good answers—one man put it to me straight: "Who is the government?" he asked. The question was only two words long in Arabic, but I had to ask him to repeat it a couple of times before I understood what he was getting at.

Who *was* the *government?* Who was in charge in Iraq? So far as this man could see, there were occasional Humvees rolling through the streets, but no one was in charge. "Well," I told him after a painful pause, "Ambassador Bremer is the government." "Oh," he said, apparently satisfied. He gave no indication of having heard of Bremer, who had arrived less than a week before. "So long as someone is in charge." Then, as if on cue, automatic weapons fire broke out. The kids in the crowd around us scattered, which was conventionally thought to be a good proxy for whether the bullets were headed in your direction or not. The men ambled off, and my Airborne friends and I did exactly what the rulebook told us to do under those conditions. We took cover, if you can call it that when you are exposed on a city sidewalk. When the shooting died down, my buddy, Captain Kobey Langley, gave the order "Haul ass." And we did, running unceremoniously to our Humvees and taking off, tires screeching.

When no one is in charge, you need protection. Scores of would-be political parties sprang up—more than a hundred in the first two post-Saddam months alone. Civil society *in potentia* was there. But these were new parties, untested and untried, and no one had heard of them. Far more reliable as guarantors of collective security were associations forming around denominational identity. The Shi'i clergy stepped right in, promoting the interests of their community and immediately starting to build civil society on the foundation of the religious institutions that they now controlled by default. They did not adopt oppositional rhetoric to begin with. In fact, outside mosques all over Baghdad in May and June 2003, you could see enormous black bedsheets inscribed with the rhyming couplet "Not Sunni, not Shi'i—Islamic unity!" But the implicit assumption of these messages was that Sunni and Shi'i were the default identities to which people would probably have recourse, and that universalizing Islamic identity should be used to find common ground between them. Soon Sunnis were following suit in the identity game, and a subset of them were justifying their insurgency—in its own distorted way, a form of mutual protection—in terms of the collective self-interest of the Sunni community.

The critics of the CPA, from both inside and outside Iraq, are therefore slightly misstating the case when they blame the recognition of denominationally based political associations for reifying Shiʿi and Sunni identity and thus dividing the country. In fact the CPA was woefully unprepared for the degree to which Shiʿi denominational identity became so central to the political future of the country. Neoconservative advocates of war, encouraged by Iraqi exiles, mistakenly expected that secular Iraqi national identity would prevail over Shiʿi sectarianism.

Denominational identity emerged not *because* of CPA recognition but despite its delay, and for reasons having everything to do with the need for mutual protection and the advantages of identity-based groups in providing it. It would be perfectly correct, however, to blame the invasion for creating a situation in which a pervasive sense of insecurity quickly descended upon Iraqi life, necessitating in short order the formation of protection associations other than the state. In that indirect but nonetheless decisive sense, the Coalition, specifically the United States, played a major role in the rapid emergence of denominational identities in the immediate postwar period. The United States did not invent those identities, nor did it intentionally reify them; but it produced an environment in which it was necessary for Iraqis to invent them. Had there been half a million U.S. troops on the ground, it is highly likely that there would have been little looting, no comparable sense of insecurity, and therefore a reduced need for denominational identities to become as dominant as they quickly did.[31]

The first duty of a nation-building power, then, is to produce order in the very literal sense of monopolizing violence. The international community signally failed to accomplish this goal in Somalia, and that is the main reason why Somalia remains today not a state but rather a congeries of disparate groups, each with its own warlord.[32] In Iraq, this goal was never fully accomplished during the occupation. The absence of civil society in Iraq, coupled with the perceived anarchy in the period just following the fall of Saddam's regime, created conditions in which denominational identities showed themselves in ways that were profoundly detrimental to security. The Sunni insurgency, I have suggested, is best understood through the lens of Sunnis' concern about their future in an Iraq where Shi'is and Kurds dominate. While the Shi'a did not engage in inter-communal violence, they did form militias, and violence would become very likely if the Shi'a perceived a risk that the United States would walk away from Iraq without being replaced by some other stabilizing military or quasi-military force.

The United States owed to Iraq during the occupation and beyond a duty to put down the existing insurgents and to guarantee safety and security. The former task unquestionably always had a major political component. During the occupation, many Sunnis did not see the advantages of entering into a democratic arrangement, because they feared that their minority status would ensure that they became permanent losers. The Transitional Administrative Law gave them some paper guarantees, like equal rights and a guarantee of equitable distribution of state resources (read: oil money); but legal guarantees have little sway before anyone knows whether they will be effective.

But there was also an irreducible military component to the job of ending the insurgency. The insurgents consistently attacked Iraqi civilians and Iraqi police installations. These were breaches of the peace that could not be tolerated. We were under a duty to protect the Iraqis who were the main victims of this insurgency—and that meant protecting them by force.

The Coalition's security obligation extends forward beyond just ending the insurgency, however. By its presence, even after the occupation formally ended, the Coalition was under a duty to guarantee that the country would not revert to anarchy. That means an obligation for American or international troops to remain until they can be replaced by Iraqi security forces under the command of the democratic state. Militias will not do, because, as in Somalia, they will be responsible to particular factions, and not to a central government. As a consequence, their presence is at best a very weak guarantor of law and order.[33]

The duration for which our obligation to guarantee security in Iraq will continue is a complex topic, one to which I shall return in chapter 3. For now, let me say only that a security umbrella is a necessary condition for the emergence of a democratic state. In the run-up to such a state, and indeed in the aftermath of its emergence, an element of instability will be introduced by the possibility that any one power association in the country might try to assert the capacity to oppress the others by military force.[34] If the Iraqi army had still existed during the occupation, and if it had been possible to ensure that it would not break apart or take the side of one particular faction, that military could potentially have been used to provide this security guarantee. But after the Coalition disbanded the army, it became an accomplished fact that the Iraqi military no longer existed—and there was no going back on this decision, rash and mistaken though it was. The United States now has no ethical choice but to remain until an Iraqi security force, safely under the civilian control of the government of a legitimate, democratic state, can be brought into existence.

If we can satisfy this fundamental ethical obligation—which, as I suggested, the international community did not manage to fulfill in Somalia—we could then turn to the next duty of nation building, which is to preside over the formation of the basic institutions necessary for a stable, democratic state. It is this step, more than the provision of security, which is most deeply affected by the acknowledgment that we do not know any better than do occupied peoples how exactly those institutions should be formed. In the familiar ideology and rhetoric of nation building, our expertise, derived at least in part from living in a successful democratic state ourselves, ought to be deployed to help Iraqis reach their objective. And if our collective knowledge is admitted to be inapposite, because conditions in Iraq differ so markedly from those anywhere else, then in any case we ought to send our experts, men and women who by virtue of their training or experience in nation building elsewhere know how to get things done.

Here I want to reiterate a deep skepticism about the capacity of outside experts—myself not excluded—to design democratic institutions that will work. There are simply too many instances of abject failure in the annals of nation building, perpetrated not only by the enlightened amateur postcolonialists of yesteryear but by modern experts as well. It is true that, in Germany and especially Japan, nation building from without largely succeeded.[35] But think of the counterexamples. The U.S.-trained lawyers who descended on Latin America in the 1950s and 1960s to bring with them the rule of law in the North American sense succeeded only in muddling things up.[36] In postcolonial Africa, the results were far worse.[37] Admittedly, these were typically instances of advice, not of direct imposition. But they were failures of expertise nonetheless. We like to imagine that our expertise will make the difference; in the end, though, not we, but the Iraqis, will have to run these institutions and make them work—and there is just too much that we do not understand about the complexities of Iraqi politics and society.

My skepticism, however, does not lead me to conclude that we should abandon any role in the processes whereby institutions must be designed. There is a crucial, constructive role that we can play even after we have divested ourselves of the mistaken, paternalistic, patronizing view that we know how to design institutions for the Iraqis better than they know themselves. That role derives precisely from our outsider status and our position as guarantors of security. We can, under the right conditions, serve as impartial mediators between the different factions and interest groups that are emerging in Iraqi politics; and a crucial aspect of our impartiality must be to ensure that all relevant groups get represented in that process.

We ought, in other words, to play the role of leopard-skin chief: the quasi-outsider who has no strong preference for any particular local party.[38] We are plausible candidates for this "honest broker" role for no better reason than that our main objective is establishing a state which is stable because democratically legitimate. By analogy to our role as a guarantor of security, we can guarantee that all Iraqis get a seat at the table, and we can facilitate the process of negotiation by our presence. All Iraqis, or at least all Iraqis that I have met, want Iraq to be independent and U.S. forces to leave. That desire should structure their incentives to agree upon democratic arrangements that will enable us to do just that.

There are two related temptations that we must avoid in the process of supervising negotiations over Iraq's political future. One is the temptation to put a thumb on the scales, favoring our allies at the expense of those whose interests seem at the moment to be opposed to our own. In the long run, giving advantages to our allies will have the effect of destabilizing the country that we want to see emerge.

It *is* appropriate for us to favor—not to impose—certain substantive constitutional outcomes, particularly those that guarantee equal treatment of all Iraqis, regardless of sex, religion, and so forth. But the reason to favor these outcomes must be that we believe that the vast majority of Iraqis want them. If large numbers of Iraqis disagreed, expressly preferring overt inequality, that would complicate matters considerably, forcing a direct confrontation between the principle of equality and that of self-determination that I do not propose to resolve here. Instead, I want to suggest that our outcome preference here should be no different from our general preference for the creation of a legitimate democracy in Iraq. We may be primarily motivated by our own security, but that interest is ethically defensible only if it coincides with the expressed preferences and interests of Iraqis. We can and should encourage guarantees of religious liberty. But our motivation must be that Iraq will be a more stable and secure place if religious freedom is provided. If Iraqis in fact are convinced that, say, allowing foreign religious missionaries in their country would be a threat to stability and public safety—as indeed is the (entirely plausible) concern in India, where such missionaries are typically denied resident status—then we would not be justified in insisting on a provision guaranteeing them access. Of course in principle there is no reason why Iraqis should not be able to make difficult constitutional decisions without our interference. But the reality of negotiation is that there is disagreement, sometimes profound, over fundamental questions—and in many of these it would be unrealistic for us to have no opinion at all.

The second temptation, as powerful as the first, is to adjudicate disputes among Iraqi factions when it comes to institutional design. What makes this temptation still greater is that it is only natural for some groups of Iraqis to ask the occupier to do just that, when they believe it will serve their interests. (This was a recurrent feature of the interim constitutional negotiations.) The Coalition was, after all, the most powerful force in the country. All the political actors there were constantly trying to figure out what we believed was in our interests, in order to promote their own. We can see a similar dynamic at work in, for example, Israeli-Palestinian negotiations. Often the Palestinian side sought American adjudication of thorny issues in the hope that it would yield a better outcome than would direct negotiations in which the Palestinians were inevitably the weaker party.[39]

As the power player in Iraq, the CPA was often called upon to intervene when negotiated drafts were put before it. Thus, for example, disagreement between Kurds and other Iraqis over the extent of federalism arose regularly in the TAL negotiations. The Kurds typically turned to the CPA—always assuming they thought it would agree with them—and asked it to endorse the justice of their demand for greater autonomy. As sophisticated political actors, they assumed the CPA would agree with them to the extent that agreement served the CPA's interests in resolving complex issues of negotiation and speeding up withdrawal. Perhaps the CPA wanted the Kurds to prevail on certain points; but it nonetheless should have refrained from deciding them in their favor. Ethically speaking, it was not for the CPA to resolve the dispute, though it may have appeared to be in its short-term interest to do so. Collective decisions about the future of Iraq were not the CPA's to make. Even if they were, the decisions would have had a much better chance of lasting and taking hold if made on the basis of a mutually self-interested Iraqi compromise, without direct U.S. intervention. Thus, for example, the debate over the method for ratifying the permanent Iraqi constitution is continuing, even though the TAL, as written, provided for a veto if two-thirds of the voters in three provinces refuse to ratify the constitution. From this debate the United States should have and would be well-advised to keep clear.

Of course U.S. nonintervention is to an extent a myth. The entire negotiation would not be happening if the United States had not removed Saddam and had not had troops on the ground, oil beneath their feet, and therefore, on both counts, a long-term strategic interest in the outcome. But going forward, the United States must avoid getting itself into a situation where it could have to remain in Iraq for the long haul in order to keep its favored clients in power. This, ultimately, is what must differentiate this nation-building exercise in Iraq from that of the British. The goal must be to build a machine that will run of itself, not a system in which a minority requires permanent external propping up.

My hypothesis has been that we want legitimate democracy in Iraq for the instrumental reason that it represents a form of institutionalized power sharing with the capacity to sustain itself internally. The ethical virtues of democracy matter only as a reason why such nation-building goals are permissible. Foreign troops, then, will undoubtedly have to remain in Iraq for some time, as the institutions designed by Iraqis find their sea legs. The United States should be prepared, if necessary, to intervene in Iraq's internal affairs to preserve the arrangements that Iraqis themselves have democratically reached. But we must not be there to support an oppressive minority against a justified majority. It is this commitment to ourselves—that we will support only institutional arrangements that can facilitate long-term success—that holds out the promise of an ethical exit strategy. When things are running suitably smoothly, and an international or, better, an Iraqi security force can guarantee the peace, we will be entitled—indeed obligated—to leave.

Earlier in this chapter, I posed two challenges to the trusteeship version of nation building: first, that it was hopelessly paternalistic, and second, that it was ethically untenable because of the conflict of interest that it posed for the occupier who must put the Iraqis first. I acknowledged that trusteeship has a paternalistic history, but insisted that we must abandon a paternalistic conception of trusteeship in favor of one that sees the trustee as no different from an ordinary government and eschews ambitious claims of special expertise. But what of the problem of conflict of interest? Exercising power on someone else's behalf involves daily, almost minute-by-minute divergence between the interests of the two sides.

It would be nice if we could resolve these tensions simply by asserting that we share an interest with the Iraqis in producing a stable, legitimate democracy in Iraq. That is too simple, though. It neglects the issue of the appropriate means to achieve that end, and the different power distributions that are all in principle compatible with that outcome. There *are* conflicts of interest in the nation builder's position. The nation builder wants stability and it wants out, but it wants those things for its own reasons and may not have the occupied people's interests at heart when it charts the way to democracy. Unlike the selection of objectives, which I have argued need not be motivated by the interests of those occupied, the choice of means under conditions of trusteeship does require putting the occupied people first. That is what it means to be trustee: to serve the interests of the beneficiary.

Another way to describe this problem is by historical analogy. Tension between the trustee and the beneficiaries pervaded the British mandatory experience in Iraq. The conflicting interests of the British and the Iraqis produced deep rifts that disserved the cause of nation building. Couldn't it fairly be said that the neocolonialism of nation building is doomed by the inevitability of these sorts of disagreements?

Seen in this light, the problem with modern nation building is not that it replicates the classical feature of colonialism, namely, external control over subject peoples. After all, classical colonialism involved direct rule of indefinite duration, which, despite some suspicions to the contrary, is not the American objective in Iraq. Rather, contemporary nation building reflects many of the dynamics of *late* colonialism, the phenomenon that arises when the colonial power understands it must leave for reasons of global politics or internal economic viability, but has not yet relinquished control.

Late colonialism, of course, has an end-state. The British Empire did leave Iraq, as indeed it eventually left the Raj and even, belatedly, Hong Kong. I think it is a similarly foregone conclusion that U.S. forces will eventually leave Iraq, although that could perhaps be disputed insofar as the United States still keeps some forty thousand troops in South Korea and kept a comparable number in West Germany until the Cold War ended. What matters, though, for our analysis, is how the dynamics of power operate between the nation builder and the people under occupation. Specifically, I want to address the question whether the presence of those conflicts dooms nation building as an ethical matter by making profound paternalism unavoidable.

I can state my answer to this question briefly. The power of the nation builder to make irreversible decisions with respect to the politics of the country under occupation is much exaggerated. The dominant experience of nation builders, the moment they seek to draw on the local participants in the governing process, is one of profound constraint. Power is not unidirectional but negotiated between different parties. Much to the consternation of American government officials who had not read their Foucault, negotiation is the reality of political power when nation building is taking place. The conflicts between the parties are real and undeniable, but as it turns out, the power of Iraqis in the nation-building process served as a counterweight to the ethical concern that the Coalition might entirely subordinate the Iraqis' interests to their own.

Examples could be multiplied. Ambassador Bremer declared that the interim constitution could not be too Islamic; but once he said so, Islamists redoubled their demands, and what emerged was a document that not only made Islam a source of legislation but also prohibited laws that contradict the principles of Islam on which there is consensus.[40] When the CPA declared its intention to arrest Muqtada Sadr, it turned out that actually doing so would cast the country into turmoil even greater than that created by Sadr's mini-rebellion—so the CPA backed down. De-Ba'thification was the stated CPA policy for a year, but when the Sunni insurgency got bad enough, the CPA shifted gears and rehabilitated many ex-Ba'thists.

I do not mean to say, then, that there is no conflict-of-interest problem in nation-building trusteeship. The British under the mandate, no different from the CPA, faced the formidable ethical hurdle of putting Iraqis' interests before their own. The British demonstrated a marked tendency to fall down on the job in this respect, and the CPA showed many signs of doing the same. All I mean to argue is that the power Iraqis actually have in the nation-building process suggests that the occupier's conflict of interest is not an insuperable obstacle, just a tall one.

If nothing stands in the way of my doing exactly as I please, it will be very hard indeed for me to constrain myself to put your interests first. I would have to be so ethically scrupulous that I might qualify as a saint. And saints we assuredly are not. Yet if you are capable of pushing back against me, I do not need to be quite as pure to ensure that I consider your interests. You will be there to keep me honest, and I will end up spending a great deal of my time trying to figure out just what your interests are and how they interact with my own. I might still fail to put your interests first, but it is a fair bet that I will have given them some thought.

Running the daily affairs of Iraq, even through a complex model of power sharing, produced serious disagreements between the interests of the occupiers and those of the Iraqis. To explore the dynamics of power more fully, however, would require a deeper inquiry into the question of who the CPA's interlocutors in Iraq were—and who they were not. We have already had occasion to speak of Ayatollah ʿAli Sistani, who did not himself hold any official position in the apparatus created to handle the transfer of power from the CPA to Iraqis. I have in mind specifically the members of the Governing Council, the transitional ministers whom they selected, and the transitional authority that assumed nominal sovereignty on June 30, 2004.

Considering the way these figures acquired power, and how they deployed what power they had vis-à-vis the CPA, will shed further light on the limits to the occupier's power and its relation to the ethics of nation building. It will also serve as an effective opening to the question of elections and the closely related problem of when it will be practically possible and ethically acceptable for the U.S. forces to leave Iraq once and for all. The next and final chapter will be devoted to these important matters.

Let me leave you with a few final thoughts about internationalization, the option urged by Democrats[41] throughout the occupation period, and to a degree embraced by the Bush administration as the occupation waned. Trusteeship and paternalism are difficult to disentangle, and that alone might be reason enough to doubt the ethical viability of nation building in a post–Cold War world. But how much of our instinctive objection to trusteeship derives from skepticism about the legitimacy of the invasion of Iraq and the consequent illegitimacy of the U.S.-led occupation? We are, I suspect, more comfortable with the notion of a de facto trusteeship for Kosovo, run initially by the redoubtable Bernard Kouchner, a founder of Médecins Sans Frontières and a living symbol of well-meaning international assistance,[42] or for East Timor under the late Sergio Vieira de Mello.[43] The Kosovo bombing seems to have been morally justified on grounds of intervention in ethnic cleansing (even though the Security Council initially vetoed it). The involvement of the international community and the imprimatur of the United Nations after the fact make us think that the occupier is authorized to rule, by necessity if by nothing else.

Yet the paternalism and conflicts of interest inherent in trusteeship apply with no less force to an internationally authorized nation-building project than they do to one undertaken unilaterally.[44] The international community, too, takes on the burdens of nation building in a neo-Wilsonian spirit of doing for others what they cannot do themselves. An international presence offers but a weak check on the tendency of nation-building administrators to act more in their own interests than in those of the country they are rebuilding.[45] UN-appointed transitional administrators are, in principle, exposed to the criticism of the community of nations. In practice, though, they can and do countermand local political preferences with little worry that anyone who matters will object. The administrators themselves have career advancement interests; and the UN bureaucracy from which many spring has its own distinctive set of concerns, practices, and habits. Finally, the UN reflects the interests of *its* member states, which need not coincide with those of the people subject to administration. The United Nations may be better in this respect than the League that preceded it, but in both cases the patina of international legitimacy will often hide the de facto dominance of one particular country or group of countries in the process of nation building.

I urge, then, the value of considering nation building in Iraq on its own terms, notwithstanding one's views on the war that gave rise to it, or the question of who is doing the administering. Internationalizing the nation-building process in Iraq was always highly desirable as a political matter, but it would neither have reduced the ethical burden on the United States nor alleviated the concerns associated with trusteeship as a viable ethical model for nation building. The question of just international intervention, as I suggested earlier, is enormously important. But if we indulge in the luxury of condemning the nation-building project in Iraq just because we object to how we got there, we may miss the point of the ethical obligations that still stare us in the face. We got ourselves— and the Iraqis—into a serious fix: and we must see it through.

CHAPTER THREE

The Magic of Elections and the Way Home

DURING HIS YEAR AS CIVIL ADMINISTRATOR IN BAGHDAD, L. Paul Bremer gave regular press conferences in front of a rather amateurish emblem of the Coalition Provisional Authority that hung on the wall of his favored venue, the largest meeting room in a building known as the Iraqi Forum. That spot had a history. When I first entered the Forum, on April 28, 2003, the place subsequently occupied by the large, oval-shaped insignia featured a rectangular discoloration where a large portrait of Saddam Hussein had hung until just days before. Beneath the blank space was a verse from the Qur'an in elegant calligraphy: "Consult the people regarding the matter," advised the verse, "and when you have reached a decision, then put your trust in God."[1]

In a sense, no verse could have been more appropriate for the April meeting I was attending, in which some three hundred Iraqis from all over the country had been gathered to discuss the future of the country in the immediate aftermath of the American invasion, before the CPA had been formed. Along with a second verse that also praises consultation[2]—*shura* in Arabic—the verse on the wall in front of us was often invoked by advocates and activists to claim Qur'anic authority for democratic institutions. For what is consultation in today's world, they ask, if not electoral democracy? And what point to consultation if those consulted cannot remove leaders who fail to heed them? Needless to say, Saddam had no such interpretation in mind when he had the verse inscribed beneath his image. He presumably intended a reading according to which he was engaging in consultation with his subjects before taking decisions that were then to be understood as authorized by God. But in the heady first days after Saddam's fall, with the appointment of an American civil administrator to oversee the occupation still just an unrealized contingency, the verse seemed as though it might be a harbinger of new, democratic developments.

As it turned out, Saddam's portrait was not the only design element removed from the front wall in the Iraqi Forum meeting room to make way for the CPA logo. The Qur²anic verse calling for consultation went, too. Without making too much of the symbolism, one might note the parallel between the wall decor and the structure of political authority. In late April 2003, it could still be fantasized that some quasi-spontaneous democratic order might emerge, phoenix-like, from the rubble of the Baᶜthist state, embodying the divine directive of consultation. Within a month, however, the disorganization and institutional unrootedness of meetings like the one held on April 28 had given way to a top-down occupation authority headed by an administrator who was, in practice if not in name, viceroy of Iraq. His insignia was not his face but a bland graphic, designed to evoke, somewhat hopefully, the boring regularity of bureaucratic control and the end of Saddam-style personal rule.³ The verse had to go. Elections, at least for the moment, were off the table. Nation building had begun.

The paradox of nation building cannot be put more pointedly than by stating the problem of elections. According to the hypothesis I have been developing over the last two chapters, the desired outcome of nation building is a legitimate, democratic government that respects citizens' equality and individual rights. Such a democracy must, according to a conventional understanding that obtains from Rio de Janeiro to Stockholm to Mumbai, feature free, competitive elections to be worthy of the name. But if elections could be held the day that the old government fell, and if those elections could produce a government capable of monopolizing violence and ruling through law, then nation building would be unnecessary. Nation building is called for precisely where instant elections are not a realistic option.[4]

The goal of nation building, then, is to produce conditions suitable for democratic elections without initially holding such elections. To say this is a delicate business is to understate the case significantly. Elections for a government that actually rules form a crucial—probably the most crucial—building block in the production of democratic legitimacy. The legitimacy of the end-state that nation building seeks to create will therefore turn on the holding of elections. Nation building seeks to generate an end-state of legitimacy, then, without deploying the most potent source of such legitimacy.

Instead, the nation-building project treats the important subject of elections through a mechanism of deferral—one might almost say, of *différance*. The ideology of nation building holds out the prospect of a future moment at which the structure of government will be fundamentally altered from the one that prevails during the period of nation building: democratic instead of undemocratic; fully participatory instead of consultative at best. In so describing the world, the ideology of nation building implicitly recognizes the illegitimacy of the structure of governance that prevails prior to those elections. In this way, nation building undercuts itself by denying its own legitimacy.

Yet at the same time, nation building affirms its own absolute necessity to produce the conditions of legitimacy that lie just ahead, out of reach. Like the metaphor Wittgenstein proposes in the *Tractatus*, nation building presents itself as a ladder whose rungs disappear as the climber leaves each one behind.[5] Its own obsolescence built into its structure, nation building aspires to consume itself.

At the same time, elections can also seduce with the promise of release. The siren of elections calls out to both the nation builder and the nation being built, even if each hears her song differently. Elections hold out the hope of successful consummation, the seed of democracy implanted and the door opened for subsequent withdrawal. In this troubling vision the occupied people grip the occupier in an embrace both pleasurable and terrifying. In the imagined "successful" scenario, the occupier builds and leaves. When things go wrong, he cannot get out but is sucked into what American vernacular tradition calls "the quagmire"—a situation from which he cannot extract himself, but in which he cannot remain without suffering unmanning damage. On this reading, Vietnam is the archetype of failure, and the angular cut into the ground that is the famous Vietnam Memorial in Washington, D.C., takes on a new and disturbing significance.

From the perspective of the nation under occupation, elections seduce in a different sort of way. On one hand, they promise to give voice to the voiceless. In Arabic, as in many other languages, the word for "vote" is the word for "voice." To speak, in this conception, is to take responsibility for one's future, and to engage in the act of self-determination that is, in Wilsonian terms, the nation's very reason for being. In that same moment of self-creation, what is more, the nation being built can throw off the yoke of its occupier and declare its independence, thus breaking free of the humiliating status of being subordinated.

On the other hand, people under nation building fear elections for the danger of what they may reveal. Fragmented results may show that there is no nation there at all, just a collection of divergent interest groups who lack the common vision to make a government that will endure.[6] The election of undemocratic forces is also to be feared.[7] It is not only Westerners who worry that free elections in Islamic countries might yield the result of one man, one vote, one time.[8] Electoral results like these would not just short-circuit the nation-building process symbolically. They could well destroy it practically, as well. If, in the aftermath of elections, citizens are not confident that some sort of basically legitimate, cooperative government will emerge, then they will not wait until disaster is upon them to protect themselves. They will coalesce, or perhaps recoalesce, into the mutual protection associations that I described in the previous chapter. Based on whatever forms of allegiance lie closest at hand, and driven by a prisoner's-dilemma logic of self-preservation, these protection associations will sprout militias and eye one another warily, or worse. The result will be democratic government stillborn, the attempt to produce a nation thwarting even the emergence of an effective state.

It should not be surprising, then, that elections, with their magic, their mystery, and their danger, nearly obsess the process of nation building. Various internationally administered transitional administrations have tried, with limited success, to use elections alongside the ultimate veto power of the foreign administrator.[9] By contrast, in Iraq, the foreign administrator left before national or meaningful local elections occurred, with nominal sovereignty passing to an unelected Iraqi transitional government on June 28, 2004. In either situation, elections are conceived as central. Having gestured toward how elections suffuse the theory and practice of nation building, I would now like to propose a revisionary, chastened, and I hope ethically responsible account of how elections should be deployed in nation building so as to help create democratic legitimacy, and of the relation between elections and the end-state of nation building.

My thesis can be stated briefly. Too much has been made of the redemptive power of elections, and too little of their capacity to check the arbitrary exercise of power. Beginning with nonelective consultative structures, nation builders should try to establish mechanisms of responsiveness to popular sentiment in countries being built. Elections for a government should then follow, *but not as the end point of nation building.* When an elected government is in place, nation building will ordinarily have just begun. The nation builder will still have the ethical responsibility to preserve order and devote further resources to institutional development until an elected government is actually able to exercise the powers of sovereignty. These include the protection of borders without and the maintenance of law and order within. Once a legitimate, democratic government does exercise actual sovereignty, not just a paper version, the nation builder is ethically bound to withdraw its forces unless the new government asks it to remain involved as a guarantor of continuing security. If such a request is forthcoming, it, too carries ethical weight: the nation builder cannot defensibly ignore this request. If the new nation wants its help to preserve stability through military presence, the nation builder has no ethical choice but to remain.

The crucial point I wish to emphasize is that elections are not a ticket home for the nation builder, nor are they the magic bullet of true sovereignty for the nation being built. My claim rests on a descriptive account of what actually happens when elections take place; on a theoretical criticism of the way the concept of sovereignty has been deployed in the discussion of nation building in Iraq; and on an interpretation of the ethical responsibilities of a nation builder that has taken on a transformative task, creating high risks for the people whose institutions are being altered.

Let me begin, then, by addressing the hard practical question of what elections actually can accomplish. In so doing, I hope to deflate some of the grand visions associated with electoral democracy, which ironically are shared both by its advocates and by some of its most sophisticated detractors. On my account, under conditions of nation building, elections can inject elements of responsiveness and accountability into ordinary politics. This makes elections a more important check on the interests of the nation builder than we are sometimes willing to admit. But elections do not often express "the will of the people," as exponents in a broadly Rousseauian tradition would claim. Neither do they necessarily empower dictatorships of the majority that in turn threaten the life, liberty, and property of vulnerable minority groups, as skeptics of democratization have variously argued.

The easiest way to tell this story is by laying out briefly and schematically the two opposing sides of the argument about elections and nation building. One view about elections in the nation-building process holds that direct elections should be held as soon as practicable, in order to bring the broad public into its proper position of sovereignty. The strongest basis for this argument is that the unelected nation-building authority does not, on its own, possess sufficient incentives to act in a way that is responsive to public desires and accountable to popular judgment. A weaker justification—but one always present in the public mind—is that nation building should move as swiftly as possible toward normal democratic government, which certainly involves elections. This view prevailed in post–Cold War nation-building exercises in Bosnia and East Timor. In Timor it worked reasonably well;[10] but in Bosnia it created major problems when antidemocratic forces were elected.[11] In Kosovo, imagined as a variant, the international administrator holds elected officials in check by a judicious use of his veto and direct command powers, a solution satisfactory, it would seem, to no one.[12]

The alternative view, which in its most recent incarnation grows out of the Balkans failures, worries that in early elections, the wrong people get elected. The "wrong people" include rump elements of the former, removed regime, who oppose nation building and want primarily to reinstate their previous power; and they also include antidemocratic forces who win votes on the basis of widespread dissatisfaction. In Bosnia, the wrong people meant recalcitrant Serbian nationalists. In Iraq, the wrong people were thought to include former Ba'thists who aspired to reestablish Sunni dominance, or radical Islamists like Muqtada Sadr who openly rejected the entire notion of democracy as un-Islamic. A further reason for delaying elections in Iraq, according to the antielections view, was that almost everywhere in the Arab world where relatively free elections had been held after a long period of secularist autocracy, Islamist political parties had enjoyed remarkable success. The most prominent example was that of Algeria, where free elections following thirty years of a revolutionary—roughly speaking, socialist—dictatorship yielded a massive victory for the Islamist Front Islamique du Salut, after which the military called off the elections, jailed the Islamist leadership, and plunged the country into a bloody, decade-long civil war.[13]

Both of these views have some real measures of truth to them. A rush to elections is extremely risky under postconflict nation-building conditions. If the long-term goal is the production of a stable, legitimate, democratic government, there really is reason to approach the timing of elections very cautiously. This stance may sound paternalistic; but recall that the very reason we need nation building in any particular case is precisely that immediate post-conflict elections are not feasible. It would indeed be paternalistic if one were to argue that elections are *never* appropriate in nation building, or that the public ought to have *no* say in the major decisions taken by the nation-building power. But to say that electoral results will differ depending on the contingent political and economic circumstances is not an insult but an accurate description of reality. If James Carville was stating a truth about the electoral realities of the 1992 U.S. presidential election when he coined the aphorism "It's the economy, stupid," then in the context of any election we can fairly predict that there are certain issues that will predominate. What is more, the initial endowments of different political bodies competing for electoral power differ dramatically.

The longer one waits after the collapse of the old order to hold elections, the more opportunity for new political associations and ideas to emerge.

Yet it is also unquestionably true that the mechanisms of free speech and assembly, which I discussed in the previous chapter as crucial to supervising the nation builder's efforts, on their own cannot do the same job that elections can in holding government to account. There is a reason that modern democracies universally rely on elections to change governments. It is not that elections do an especially good job of identifying some idealized general will. In fact, in most true democracies, election results tend to be relatively close, and major political shifts occur infrequently.[14] Nor do elections provide fine-grained accountability or responsiveness with respect to particular issues. Congress is charged with such an enormous range of responsibility that, even if I vote primarily on environmental issues, enough other people will vote on their particular issues that the results can rarely be scrutinized for a hidden message about how my congressman should vote on the environment. The exercise of speech—along with, in our bizarre American system, the expenditure of campaign-finance funds—is the tool of choice for fine-grained policy promotion.

Elections, rather, do two things well. First, they provide large-scale accountability. Elections answer the question "Is the government, overall, doing a good enough job from my perspective to deserve to remain in power?"[15] The importance of this question cannot be overstated. In the model of political authority as trusteeship, it corresponds to the question that the supervisors of the trust should be asking themselves: Is the trustee serving the beneficiaries' interests? If it appears that, to the contrary, the trustee is serving his own interests, the supervisors—ordinarily, the electorate—can kick the bums out. The nation builder will not stand directly for election, so it follows as a matter of course that he can never be as accountable as elected politicians can be. This is an identifiable, nonmystical reason for transferring as much power as possible from the nation builder to an elected government as soon as feasible.

The second thing elections do relatively well is reveal, albeit in fuzzy snapshot form,[16] public preferences about *whose* views, very generally speaking, ought to be followed in government. The analogy here is to the market, which does a better job than any other mechanism—though not a perfect job, to be sure—in revealing the important information of who values which goods, and how much.[17] If the collapse of communism demonstrates one thing, it is that central planners cannot do as good a job of guessing at such information as can the decentralized market in making that information manifest. Similarly, the guesses of leaders and politicians about what the public wants are less reliable than elections, in which people cast their votes and hence manifest their preferences much as we do when we open our pocketbooks. Modern polling methods, like modern market research, have the sophistication to tell us much more than was ever imagined possible about voter preferences. But in the end, there is no substitute for putting your money, or your vote, where your mouth is. The pollster's questionnaire is dress rehearsal for the ballot box.

A nation builder, even one that draws on the best in modern polling,[18] operates under a debilitating uncertainty about what different members of the public actually want. In this sense, the nation builder is like the communist central planner, guessing how much wheat or steel the nation will want five years hence. The nation builder, in other words, is flying blind when it comes to decisions that must be accepted by the overwhelming majority of citizens. It would be one thing if the shaping of institutions were an exercise with right answers that could be applied everywhere. If that were so, the views and opinions of the people under occupation might be irrelevant to nation building's most fundamental tasks. But of course the opposite is true. The most important facet of institution building is that the institutions coming into existence correspond to the interests of the vast majority of citizens as those citizens see them. Public opinion is nowhere more important; and without elections, it is hard to know what public opinion is.[19]

To see why this is so, consider the problem of Sunni leadership in Iraq during the occupation. With the collapse of the Ba'th Party, no voice for the Sunnis remained; and no new, easily identifiable leadership came suddenly to the fore. As a result, no one particularly knew how most Sunnis felt about the future, except that they were worried and angry. One could predict theoretically that if their uprising came to seem fruitless, they would gradually be willing to enter into democratic arrangements in which their rights would be ensured by the creation of institutions in which their voices would count; but perhaps, on the ground, Sunnis might not trust such institutions and so might have no interest in joining them. Elections in Sunni areas would reveal relevant information, likely involving competition between leaders who advocated joining such institutions and others who rejected them. The people would vote, and someone would win, by some knowable margin. The information thus revealed might not be fine-grained, but coarse-grained information would be considerably better than none, and it would empower the elected leaders to act on the basis of public opinion, democratically expressed.

It therefore follows that, in the hard work of nation building—the shaping of institutions that can be trusted by various factions in society—elections can play a tremendously valuable role. In particular, elections on this view might be especially valuable in choosing the body to draft a constitution for popular ratification. A written constitution aspires to memorialize a broad-based agreement among different segments of society about how they will structure institutions so that they may live in relative peace. To work in the long run, it therefore needs to be shaped initially by persons who can actually speak for the constituencies whose interests need to be expressed. If it turns out that elections are the only way to generate leadership that speaks for the citizens in this manner, then elections for a constituent assembly should precede constitution drafting. The pressing concern here is not the accountability function of elections but rather their information-revealing function.

The arguments that I have just sketched in favor of and against elections under conditions of nation building have in common that they resist what one might call the grand electoral narrative, according to which the act of collective voting empowers the People to take permanent decisions with unique qualities of national consensus or moral force. I do not mean to claim here that what Bruce Ackerman has famously called "constitutional moments" do not or cannot occur, for I believe that they can.[20] Multiple political forces can indeed coalesce in moments of energized collective decision that legitimately shape polities going forward. I do want to suggest, however, that elections under nation building are relatively unlikely to produce constitutional moments in this normative sense.[21] If political unity were easily achieved, nation building would hardly be necessary. A first free election is symbolically important, of course, and one can generally expect high turnout and some real debate, at least much more than in subsequent elections. The psychological stakes are high.[22] But even first elections involve ordinary people trying to choose leaders who, they fervently hope, will do right by them. Lots of voters will also cast their ballots strategically, to defend themselves against other voting blocs that might be out to achieve dominance at their expense. An outcome of divided government is far more likely than one of substantial collective will of the kind necessary to justify momentous constitutional change in Ackerman's sense.

A national referendum on whether to approve or reject a draft constitution is different. Here, with just a single question before the voter, the issue has been narrowed, and it is altogether more plausible to imagine that national self-definition is at stake. But a vote to

choose one's representative in a constituent assembly, to say nothing of a vote for one's representative in the nation's first parliament,
lacks such extraordinary qualities. It is, in the end, just a vote for
just another politician—likely to be neither more nor less important
than any other. Even someone running to serve in the constituent
assembly probably plans to run for something else afterward, if history is any judge.

But if there is something deflationary about setting aside the
great drama of the once-and-for-all-time election, there is also reason for relief in this modesty. In the last couple of years, Amy Chua[23]
and Fareed Zakaria[24] have written widely read and much praised
books sounding notes of caution—in rather different keys, I might
add—about the project of democratization. Both of these accounts
have been read, not altogether fairly, as making elections the bête
noir stalking successful democratic development, since both authors are committed advocates of liberal individual rights. For Chua,
elections bring to power ethnic majorities who threaten what she
calls "market-dominant minorities" with expropriation and violence. Zakaria, for his part, warns against the emergence of "illiberal
democracies" that do not respect the bourgeois individual rights on
which markets and liberal societies are built. I want to suggest that,
as conventionally interpreted, these two cautionary narratives place
more explanatory weight on elections than they need to bear, and
that a chastened, down-to-earth understanding of elections under
nation building can help us reevaluate some of the important fears
that Chua and Zakaria raise.

Begin with the danger of expropriation and the vulnerability of
rich minorities. Chua is unquestionably correct in identifying the
enormous risks to property owners under conditions of fundamental political change. One might quibble with her emphasis on ethnic
minorities, pointing out that property owners have been expropriated without regard to ethnicity in transitional, revolutionary
contexts ranging from the French Revolution to the Russian to
North Korea. A class-based massacre of genocidal scale—without

ethnic specificity—took place in Cambodia under Pol Pot.[25] Apparently we need no ethnic differences to rob and kill our neighbors on a massive scale. But market-dominant ethnic minorities are doubly vulnerable in their double difference, a claim that can be borne out by reference, say, to South Asian entrepreneurs in East Africa in the 1970s.

Yet it is worth considering the possibility that elections (which Chua correctly identifies as the key element of U.S.-led democratization efforts)[26] are not in themselves the crucial variable in the vulnerability of market-dominant minorities. It is, rather, the transfer of power away from elites who rely on these minorities that puts them in harm's way. There are numerous instances of market-dominant minorities losing their property and even their lives when power shifts and government changes from one form to another, not only from dictatorship to democracy. In Weimar Germany, democratic liberalism allowed Jews to flourish, while National Socialism heralded their destruction. Idi Amin was no democrat, illiberal or otherwise, when he came to power by military coup and dispossessed property-owning South Asians in Uganda. There are also counterexamples, such as that of South Africa, where democratization did not herald expropriation. My point is that democratization does create risks for market-dominant minorities, but it does so as a local example of a broader phenomenon in which political change creates new vulnerability for property owners by holding out the possibility of radical redistribution.

Elections, then, are not the big worry for market-dominant minorities under conditions of nation building. The mere fact of political change is the cause for major concern—and that concern is both well-taken and inevitable. A new government, even one that emerges from the nation-building process with strong guarantees of liberal rights, may take a very different view of wealth distribution from the one that preceded it. Sunni domination of resource allocation in Baʿthist Iraq is the only Iraqi phenomenon that might be vaguely analogized to the case of a market-dominant minority.[27]

Today, Sunni Arabs are indeed worried that democracy will distribute wealth and government largesse differently in the country—a worry that is fully justified. But that would hardly count as an argument against elections, since it is up to *any* government to decide what economic arrangements will prevail and how wealth should be distributed. The prior distributive arrangements in Iraq were plainly unjust; but so, obviously enough, is wealth distribution in the Philippines and most other places where market-dominant minorities are in danger. Chua, for her part, favors wealth redistribution—and that redistribution might well be generated by a political system chosen through elections.[28]

A similar argument applies to Zakaria's reasonable concerns about the rise of illiberal democracy. Without guarantees of basic rights, a society will have no claim to be just, and it is also likely to be ill run. Illiberal democracy therefore should not be a desired end-state of nation building—and no nation builder with any common sense treats it as a goal. But even on Zakaria's view, it is not that *elections* in particular lead to illiberalism. As he acknowledges, there are many more illiberal autocracies in the world than illiberal democracies; and this is so, no doubt, for the simple reason that in any democracy in which leaders are accountable to their citizens, there will be at least *some* public demand for basic individual rights. By contrast, in autocracies, the absence of accountability gives the leader means, opportunity, and motive to deny liberal rights without compunction. It is true that some autocrats adopt the strategy of protecting small minorities so as to have easily tractable allies. Saddam, for example, "protected" Iraqi Christians even as he gassed the more threatening Kurds. But autocrats rarely confer liberal rights except in narrow, usually economic, self-interest; and they retain, or hope to retain, the power to retract those rights when convenient. Singapore, though in some sense liberal, is not likely to stop being autocratic under its present command structure.

In other words, Zakaria's classic, Madisonian concern about the tyrannical majority's denying liberal rights and oppressing minorities[29] depends on a relatively unusual version of what elections can do. In his depiction, the electoral majority speaks with a single voice of communal solidarity and self-interest, and has the capacity to enforce its will. This outcome is not unheard-of—the Bharatiya Janata Party in India may possibly be a case in the making, as Zakaria suggests—but it is extremely rare, especially in states dependent on power-sharing arrangements for their structure. In India's spring 2004 elections, the BJP was displaced from power by the old Congress Party, at least in part because of the perception that it was insufficiently focused on serving India's disparate constituencies. So a Shiʿi electoral majority in Iraq could in theory demand a constitution drastically restricting liberal rights, in apparent fulfillment of the tyranny of the majority. But to do so, the Shiʿa would have to be able to suppress the contrary interests of other Iraqis, which would be possible only if the state's security forces were fully responsive to the Shiʿa-dominated government. Although it is not impossible that some Shiʿis might initially entertain this delusion, believing that the bare fact of their constituting a majority will win them the allegiance of state institutions, it could not withstand constitutional deliberations, much less actual practice. To govern in the real world, the Shiʿa will need to form a coalition that includes Sunnis and Kurds who would otherwise go to the streets. Elections in Iraq therefore are unlikely to produce majoritarian tyranny. They are more likely to pull Iraq apart than to catapult the Shiʿa into domination.

So where are we left by this realistic account of what elections can and cannot do under conditions of nation building? I said that both views, the one that calls for elections as soon as practicable, and the one that seeks to delay elections as long as possible, possess a measure of wisdom. Although no single formula can dictate the right answer, the guiding principle must be the one I articulated a bit earlier. Elections can facilitate accountability and responsiveness, but they are not the end point of nation building.

To see how and why this is true, we need a concrete assessment of the particular circumstances obtaining in the country under discussion, and then we need to reason out a view of how elections should function in the nation-building process. I am now going to turn, as I have throughout these chapters, to the example of Iraq to provide some insight into how such decisions can and should be made in practice. To analyze the elections question in Iraq, we should begin by getting a fuller picture of the institutions and players that were involved in the debate there during the occupation period. In the two previous chapters, I have said a good deal about Ayatollah ʿAli Sistani, the Kurdish political parties, and the CPA. I have said little, though, about the official institutional framework through which Iraqi politicians operating on the national stage encountered the occupation. That framework was the Governing Council, and to it I now turn.

In the snowy January of 2004, I was sitting snugly in my New York office when the phone rang. Was it true, a journalist wanted to know, that the Iraqi Governing Council had abolished the Iraqi family law and replaced it with the shariʿa? Like most rumors connected to the activities of the Governing Council, this one had a kernel of truth to it. Earlier that month, in Decision 137, the Governing Council had voted, by a small majority and without either discussion or the appearance of the matter on its agenda, in favor of repealing the Iraqi Law of Personal Status of 1959 and replacing it with a provision that would have governed matters of marriage, divorce, and inheritance according to the school of Islamic law to which the individual adhered. Decision 137 had been criticized by women's groups in Iraq and in the Iraqi secularist press, and as a result the story had been picked up by some astute Western journalists.

But despite the natural impulse to conclude that this was the first step in the rise of theocracy in Iraq, this was one of those legal matters in which, as Justice Oliver Wendell Holmes once memorably put it, a page of history is worth a volume of logic.[30] The Personal Status Law, as written, was already based largely on shariᶜa principles.[31] In other words, Islamic law already governed family matters in Iraq, and had done so under the secularist governments of the revolutionary period and the Baᶜthist regime. The shariᶜa was not suddenly, for the first time, being introduced into the law of personal status.

The overwhelming motivation for the change was that the Personal Status Law was a unified code applying without differentiation to Shiᶜa and Sunni alike, notwithstanding differences in their legal traditions on relevant matters of personal status. The Shiᶜi clerics in Najaf had objected to the 1959 law since its initial passage on the grounds that a code restricted the jurists' independent reasoning, and that it mistakenly applied a single law to Muslims of differing sects. The code, in other words, had been extremely unpopular among some Shiᶜis for forty years. Indeed, one of the senior members of the Governing Council, the cleric Muhammad Bahr al-ᶜUlum, had as early as 1963 written a legal treatise that reviewed the Personal Status Law line by line and condemned it root and branch.[32] The desire to abolish this relic and replace it with a comparatively pluralistic model that allowed Sunnis to be governed by Sunni law and Shiᶜis to be governed by their own legal tradition when it came to family matters was therefore, unsurprisingly, high on the agenda of Shiᶜi religious leaders as soon as Saddam fell. The social meaning of the proposed change for the Shiᶜi leaders was not primarily the imposition of Islamic law where secularism had previously prevailed; it was more about the liberation of the Shiᶜa from Sunni oppression and the restoration of judicial flexibility. Identity—both denominational and professional—was more at issue than was piety.

But there was yet a further twist on the story, one directly relevant to our topic. Decision 137 had no legal force in Iraq, for the simple reason that the Governing Council as of January 2004—and this remained true throughout its tenure—had no authority to make binding laws. The laws obtaining in Iraq under conditions of occupation were those that existed the day the American tanks rolled into Baghdad, except insofar as amended by the CPA. Ambassador Bremer retained sole authority to authorize legal change in Iraq. And when Decision 137 came before him, he refused to adopt it.

The name of the Governing Council—or at least its English name, since the novel Arabic equivalent, "Council of Government" (*majlis al-hukm*), was a bit more equivocal—suggested a governing body that takes decisions. The reality, however, was somewhat different. The Governing Council governed no one. Its "decisions" were more in the nature of recommendations. While it named technocrat transitional ministers to run Iraq's various ministries, the Governing Council had little or no say in the ministries' day-to-day operations. By a November 15, 2003, agreement with the CPA, the Governing Council was given authority to draft a basic law—essentially an interim constitution—which was meant to obtain in the period from the official transfer of authority from the CPA to some Iraqi interim government until a proper constitution could be written. But even this basic law, subsequently renamed the Transitional Administrative Law, nominally had to be approved by the CPA before it could take effect.[33]

From the fact that Decision 137 had no formal legal effect in Iraq, though, one should not conclude that the decision was insignificant. By putting the proposal before Ambassador Bremer, the Shi'is on the Governing Council created a political reality in which the CPA would be compelled to respond in one way or another. In refusing to approve the proposal, Bremer communicated to Iraqis, whether Shi'i or not, that their desires would not be followed, even though a majority of the Governing Council, and probably a large majority of the Iraqi population, would have liked to see them become law. This message inevitably and incrementally undercut the CPA's authority by displaying for all to see the undemocratic nature of the occupation.

Decision 137 left Bremer with no easy choices. Had he approved it, he would have been criticized by secularist and feminist Iraqis, and probably pilloried in the American and international press for being the regressive man who enacted the shari'a in Iraq.[34] By turning it down, he strengthened support for Shi'i political groups who could present themselves to the population as standing up against the foreign occupier for what Iraqis wanted. The next time Bremer found himself negotiating with Shi'i religious leaders—something he did almost every day—he would feel pressure to give on something else, since he had been unwilling to concede on the Personal Status Law.

Thus the dynamics of power between the unelected Governing Council and the unelected Coalition Provisional Authority in Iraq. The question of what sort of legitimacy the Governing Council enjoyed in the eyes of the Iraqi public is a complex one to which we will probably never know the true answer—but let us begin by explaining where the Governing Council came from. The members of the Governing Council were selected by the Coalition to correspond in a rough demographic sense to the population of Iraq. The Council began with the leaders of five external organizations who claimed to speak for Iraqis while Saddam was still in power. Two of these, the Kurdish Democratic Party and the Patriotic Union of Kurdistan, could claim to have been chosen by the Kurdish population north of the no-fly zone in relatively free elections that took place in 1992. The other three, namely, the Iraqi National Congress, the Iraqi National Accord, and the Islamic Da'wa Party, had never stood for election for the obvious reason that they were all banned in Iraq. Like any other liberation movement based in exile—the African National Congress during apartheid is a good example—their claim to represent the citizens of Iraq depended on a negative proposition, in their case the commonsense assertion that Saddam was a totalitarian dictator who murdered and tortured on a large scale.

These organizations, and especially the Iraqi National Congress through its chairman Ahmad Chalabi, played a major role in convincing the United States to invade Iraq and remove Saddam. On the strength of this act of suasion and more than a decade of coordinated, if sometimes conflictual, political action, the exile organizations laid claim to participation in Iraqi affairs once the regime fell. The five were quickly joined by the Supreme Council for Islamic Revolution in Iraq, which although Iranian-backed had nonetheless flirted with the other organizations during the prewar period, and preferred to be included in whatever consultative or governing body the occupying authorities would form, rather than accepting the alternative of exclusion. On the urging of American interlocutors, the six groups brought in a single Sunni "independent"—as non-Ba'thists were called in Saddam's Iraq—who was a practicing lawyer in Baghdad and the son of a prominent pre–Ba'th era politician.[35]

After Saddam fell, the United States stood in a good deal of uncertainty about how to rule Iraq. This is not the place for a lengthy explanation of how the sole world superpower could find itself, having easily defeated the dictator of 25 million people, without the first clue about what to do next. Suffice it to say that the answer lay in internecine conflict within the American government, which, because it could not not agree on the purposes of the war or the actually existing conditions in Iraq, could not produce an implementable plan for what to do once the war had taken place.

One faction within the government hoped to install members of the original group of five as an interim government immediately, so that the United States would never assume civilian authority in the country. This faction hoped and expected that Ahmad Chalabi would become president of the interim government and guide the country to democracy. Comparisons with George Washington were bandied about, not altogether flippantly. Because members of this faction looked forward to an immediate civilian Iraqi authority, retired General Jay Garner was dispatched to Iraq with a mission described as "reconstruction and humanitarian assistance." The word "governance" did not figure, because Americans were not expected to govern.

As it happened, the extreme disorder of the first month of the occupation—the looting and sabotage that led to the disappearance of the apparatus of the government and the collapse of electricity and gasoline supplies—laid to rest this plan of immediate transfer to Iraqi authority. Instead the Coalition Provisional Authority was formed, with Ambassador Bremer at its head. An office of reconstruction had given way to an "Authority," and it was increasingly clear that some sort of nation building would have to happen. This new turn of events starkly posed the question of whether Iraqis would have any say in their government at all.

It took some time for an answer to emerge—and the plan changed several times afterward. The short version of the story, however, is that the CPA decided, with White House approval, to bring into being a Governing Council that would constitute a kind of compromise between Iraqi rule and an occupation run without Iraqi input. With the help of the ill-starred UN mission led by Sergio Vieira de Mello, the group of seven men who had met with Ambassador Bremer shortly after he arrived in Baghdad in May was expanded to a total of twenty-five, this time including several women. A majority of the new Council members had lived in Iraq under Saddam; but as a consequence of this fact, only one of those members, Dr. Akila Hashemi, had any recent experience serving in government. (Adnan Pachachi, literally the elder statesman of the group, had served as Iraq's foreign minister in the 1960s and had been living in exile in the United Arab Emirates since Saddam's rise to power.) The catch-22 is easy to see: on one hand, if you were involved in Iraqi politics under Saddam, you were tainted by that association, since Saddam allowed no true opposition. If, on the other hand, you were untainted, that meant you had no recent political experience and probably no political constituency.

So the appointed, handpicked members of the Governing Council were meant to stand in for the Iraqi *demos*: but they were certainly not elected. Elections were not a viable option in a country with no communications, spotty electricity, and a tenuous security situation. But that was not the only reason why the Coalition feared elections. Experiences in Bosnia loomed large, suggesting that elections held early in the nation-building cycle tended to bring to power remnants of the old regime. CPA thinking was dominated by the view that elections ought to be delayed as long as possible. In the early postwar months, it was entirely reasonable to believe that, even if high-ranking Baʿthists were barred from running in elections, low-ranking ones would run and probably win in some areas as a result of superior organization. The Baʿthists were still the only well-disciplined group in Iraq for months after the fall of Saddam—if you were at a public meeting and forty people got up and marched out in unison, you knew for certain these were the Baʿthists. No one else could get forty people to do the same thing at the same time.

What resulted from the appointment of the Governing Council was an intriguing tension arising from Council members' mix of motivations: their sincere desire to represent national Iraqi interests; their hope to act creditably and responsibly so that they would be chosen by the public in elections that must eventually be held; and their nervousness about whether they would, in fact, preserve their influence if they had to stand for election. One result of this complex of aspirations and uncertainties was that many Governing Council members never entirely gave up the thought that the Coalition might transfer sovereign authority directly to them for some interim period prior to the time the national elections could be held. Although Ambassador Bremer initially told them, in May 2003, that this outcome would never occur—at the time, he was loath to confer sovereignty on an unelected body that enjoyed no obvious national mandate—in November 2003, the Council members' hopes were renewed when the CPA announced a plan to transfer sovereignty to an Iraqi transitional government by June 30, 2004.

According to the plan, the new transitional government would not be identical to the Governing Council, or even to an expanded version of the same, but would grow from a Transitional National Assembly, to be selected by a complicated caucus process. The Governing Council members grasped immediately that the complexity of this process and its perceived opacity would make it difficult to implement. In any case, the plan would increase the likelihood of their individually remaining members of the new government without standing for general election.

Almost immediately, individual Council members began to suggest that the Governing Council should be preserved in some form in the transitional government. Some speculated that the Council could remain as a kind of appointed upper house of parliament; others, more ambitiously, suggested that if the caucus process turned out to be unworkable, the transitional government might be composed of the Governing Council itself, perhaps expanded to a larger number of members. These speculations were not idle or irrelevant. From the Council's perspective, the CPA's change in plans from May to November 2003 reflected the reality that the United States was under pressure to transfer sovereignty to Iraqis as quickly as possible. Because the CPA also feared early elections, it was not unreasonable to believe that this train of thought would lead to a transfer of power to unelected Iraqis. That, of course, was precisely what the Governing Council was: the Americans' best effort at a demographically representative, unelected Iraqi body that might nonetheless have a chance of enjoying political legitimacy in Iraq.

At this juncture, Ayatollah Sistani weighed in again, stating publicly that an interim government must be elected, not selected by caucuses with which neither he nor most ordinary Iraqis were familiar. His concern could hardly be gainsaid. Outside Iowa, almost no American could explain to you just what caucuses are or how they work. There was certainly no exact Arabic translation for the word "caucuses," which in the Arabic version of the CPA plan was rendered *mu'tamarat intikhabiyya*—"electoral conferences." If one looked closely at the proposed caucus process in Iraq, one would discover that the electors—known as the "organizing committees"—would be selected from regional and municipal councils as well as by the Governing Council itself. What all these had in common was that they had been handpicked by the Coalition, either directly by the CPA or else by local military commanders who played the major role in naming members to regional and municipal councils. Without a detailed study—which no one inside or outside Iraq, including the CPA, had made—it was literally impossible to know what sort of representational biases would emerge from the caucus process.

Now, for the first time in the American occupation of Iraq, the problem of elections was coming to a head. The Americans, squarely in the "delay elections" camp, were insisting on a transfer of sovereignty to an unelected Iraqi body, while Sistani was insisting on elections before any transfer could occur. It is important to notice that this head-to-head conflict was precipitated entirely by the American decision to insist on a June 30 transfer. Under the original American plan, Ambassador Bremer and the CPA could have remained in power until after an Iraqi government could be elected, and sovereignty could have been transferred formally to that body. Ayatollah Sistani had never challenged this plan except to demand that any constitution drafting should be performed by an elected constituent assembly. If this demand had been accommodated alongside continued CPA control, Sistani would have had no objection. But by deciding that sovereignty must formally be transferred by a date that fell before elections would be practicable, the United States had precipitated an explicit contradiction between the different possible conceptions of the role of elections in the nation-building process.

The date June 30, 2004, had, of course, no particular resonance in Iraqi consciousness or significance to the Iraqi political process, but it was comfortably in advance of the American presidential elections of November 2004. In November 2003, when the June 30 deadline was announced, it had become clear that because of security concerns, no significant number of U.S. troops could be withdrawn from Iraq prior to the American presidential elections. Thus, in the Bush administration's view, it was necessary to bring *somebody* home by summer 2004—and if it could not be the troops, it would have to be Bremer. These sorts of party-political speculations would seem to have no place in a serious discussion of the ethical duties and obligations of nation builders; but in the real world, they played their part.

As an ethical matter, it would be difficult to justify attempts to manipulate the nation-building process for domestic political gain. Of course it could be said that, without symbolic progress, the American public might have been unprepared to continue nation building, and therefore more inclined to prefer the ethically unacceptable step of immediate, unilateral withdrawal from Iraq. On this theory, bringing home the CPA might perhaps have been justified as a choice of the lesser of two evils. In any case, once the June 30 deadline had been announced and Sistani had rejected the caucuses, conflict between the two competing views of elections in nation building seemed to be almost unavoidable. What was to be done?

The ethical answer lay, I would like to suggest, in the very basic issue of how thorough a state-building job the Coalition ought to have undertaken in Iraq. On one view, nation building ought to be minimalist: build just enough institutions to enable the occupier to declare success and depart. Such institutions must be capable of avoiding immediate collapse but need not be much more durable than that. This came to be the British strategy in Iraq as it became increasingly clear to the British that their national interest would not be served by remaining for a long time; but the ultimate failure of the British strategy of minimalist nation building in Iraq does not mean we should dismiss this possibility out of hand.[36] Minimalism has, after all, significant ethical attractions. It leaves more to the autonomy of the nation being built. It exerts an independent pressure for disengagement that may help to thwart imperialist ambitions. Finally, minimalist nation building may be desired by many people who live in the occupied country.

If one were to prefer minimalist nation building in Iraq, then a strong argument could be advanced for a rapid transfer of sovereignty, to take place even before elections could feasibly be undertaken. It is true that acting with this sort of dispatch inevitably raises the tricky problem of how to ensure that the transitional government is legitimate. But this problem could conceivably have been overcome. Thus, for instance, the transitional government could potentially have been approved by a national referendum, up or down on an entire slate of candidates. Alternatively—and this was the strategy actually adopted—an unelected transitional government might be described as a caretaker pending elections, which could be held on a date less than a year away. The members of this transitional government were selected from within the GC, which managed to maintain its influence even as it was being dissolved. The offices of the new government would almost surely enjoy some first-mover advantages in the subsequent elections; yet they would also be assuming a significant risk, namely, the risk that the transitional period would go badly, and hence discredit them and harm their prospects for electability. Perhaps most important, the prospect of elections in the immediate future would render the transitional government accountable—far more so than the CPA, which never stood for elections, could ever have been.

An alternative to minimalist nation building would be more thorough without being maximalist. True maximalist nation building, of the kind that the United States undertook in Germany and Japan, may arguably be untenable for occupiers in the post–Cold War world, because of the growth of popular belief in the independent sovereignty of nations. Even in Bosnia, Kosovo, and East Timor, nominal sovereignty was never assumed by the internationally authorized transitional administration that in fact ran the show. The CPA could not have retained sovereign authority in Iraq for five or more years without being perceived, both in Iraq and elsewhere, as an empire builder rather than a nation builder. But short of maximalist nation building, there existed a more comprehensive approach that would have insisted upon retaining formal control until democratically legitimate Iraqi institutions could be formed. This was the view embodied in the original CPA plan and abandoned by the November 15, 2003, plan, which envisioned a rapid transfer of sovereignty.

Adopting a more thorough conception of nation building would have involved promising national elections for a proper transitional government as soon as practicable, presumably in winter or early spring 2005. The TAL called for exactly that, leaving uncertain the nature of the body that would govern between the planned transfer of sovereignty on June 30, 2004, and elections in January 2005. One option was to delay the transfer of sovereignty until those elections could be held. This course would have required the Bush administration to abandon the June 30 deadline—but this would hardly have been the first missed deadline in the history of the Middle East. Ayatollah Sistani might have approved this course of action, which would have represented a major setback to the members of the Governing Council who anticipated—correctly, as it turned out—playing major roles in the unelected transitional government between June 30 and the national elections six months later.

The real benefit of delaying the official transfer of sovereignty until an Iraqi-elected transitional government could have been put into place is that it would have avoided a situation in which the military power of the United States would have to be placed behind a government that could be perceived by many Iraqis as illegitimate. This scenario stood a chance of repeating some of the worst failures of nation building in the Cold War era, in which illegitimate anti-communist regimes depended on American support to survive popular resistance. If the legitimacy of the transitional government were to have been seriously challenged, the American military in Iraq would have been faced with the alternatives of letting the government try to enforce its will on its own or weighing in on the side of the transitional government put in place by the Coalition. The former course would almost certainly have meant watching the transitional government collapse. On June 28, 2004—in the event, sovereignty was transferred two days early—there had not been time for the Iraqi government to build police or other security services capable of enforcing the law. The latter course, that of military intervention, would inevitably have revealed the transitional government as an American puppet—not, perhaps, the end of the world, but calling into question the viability of subsequent Iraqi governments that are not nominally transitional. If the United States put force behind a government perceived as illegitimate, a broad-based national resistance could emerge. Intercommunal violence would follow, as Iraqis looked forward to a new round of anarchy; and 140,000 American troops would then be caught in the middle of a nightmare, the worst-case scenario for the American occupation of Iraq: Vietnam, but in Lebanon.

For the foreseeable short-term future, Coalition forces remain the only power association in Iraq capable of exercising anything like a monopoly on violence. If we admit that foreign forces will be guaranteeing the security of the country for at least the next several years, and perhaps well beyond, it follows that it is crucial for the political development of the country in those years for the government to be perceived by the broad Iraqi public as democratically legitimate. Although some challenges to the government's authority are surely inevitable, it should be possible, and it is certainly highly desirable, to avoid a situation where governmental legitimacy is impugned wholesale. In pragmatic terms, the reason political legitimacy is so important is simply that it will likely be American forces who enable the Iraqi government to call itself sovereign. In ethical terms, the reason is more or less the same: we ought not to find ourselves in a situation where we must use force of arms to impose a government that cannot lay claim to democratic legitimacy, even if that government could reasonably be defended as a necessary transitional step.

There was a natural tendency to look for the United Nations to play a role in resolving the tensions surrounding the transfer of sovereignty and the planning of elections. The latter task is one the UN does well, and several teams of electoral experts traveled to Iraq during the occupation period. Indeed, one could even imagine the argument that the United States was under an ethical duty to "internationalize" and thereby legitimize the transfer of power.

I have said relatively little about the role of the United Nations in Iraq because, in the year of occupation, and especially after the murders of Sergio Vieira de Mello and his staff in the summer of 2003, the UN's role was peripheral. The UN was gone from Iraq for most of the first year of the occupation and had only a few dozen people in the country as the occupation drew to a close. Special envoy Lakhdar Brahimi's influence on the selection of the transitional government turned out to be limited; his presence functioned as a fig leaf for a process driven by the GC and CPA. I do not doubt the value, from a narrowly American perspective, of internationalizing the foreign presence in Iraq. It was unwise, ill-considered, and expensive for the United States to keep the international community at bay from the time the occupation began. We should have done more, and sooner; and there might have been ways to do it, although getting the UN to accept Coalition protection under occupation conditions proved too difficult a task.

As an ethical matter, though, I want to sound the warning that internationalization as a solution runs the risk of being too easy. Increased internationalization, which I support and encourage, must not serve as an excuse for easy disengagement by the United States and its Coalition partners, who started the ball rolling by toppling Saddam and are therefore obligated to stick with the nation-building project to the bitter end. More important still, decisions on internationalizing or not must rest with Iraqis, not just the Coalition. Many Iraqis seemed to be deeply ambivalent about whether a UN presence would be desirable in their country. They certainly did not want sovereign or quasi-sovereign power to be assumed by anyone other than themselves. In polls, the idea of a UN-selected transitional government fared poorly.

To many of those who are committed to an international legal order, the very presence of the United States in Iraq seemed an affront, not to say a crime. But even on international-law principles, the circumstances of occupation did not allow the United States to absolve itself simply by "turning Iraq over to the UN," whatever that might mean. The occupier's duties remained until a proper, legitimate sovereign could be put in place. Ethically speaking, this responsibility is even greater than it is in legal terms. One cannot emphasize the point too strongly: an elected, sovereign government is not enough. The new elected government of Iraq must be able to exercise sovereignty in fact as well as in law before the nation builder's duties begin to lift.

Acknowledging that U.S. military presence will sustain any sovereign Iraqi government for the next several years calls for an honest evaluation of the concept of sovereignty itself as it is deployed in the context of nation building—and this evaluation should springboard us into a discussion of the crucial ethical question of when the Coalition may justifiably leave Iraq altogether. What did it mean when the occupation authorities said that they intended to "transfer sovereignty" to an Iraqi government? The formulation assumed that, during the occupation, sovereignty rested with the CPA. But by whose authority did it do so, and in what sense?

As a matter of international law, under the old terms of the Hague regulations, sovereignty was treated as a descriptive concept corresponding to who actually exercised power. Thus the duties of the occupying power specified in the Hague regulations take effect when sovereignty has "in fact" come into the hands of the occupier.[37] This account of sovereignty was of a piece with the regulations' model of trusteeship. The occupying sovereign held the country and its people in trust for the original sovereign. Under this essentially predemocratic worldview, sovereignty simply belonged to the power in charge.

The Wilsonian trusteeship model of the League of Nations Covenant complicated matters, because it implied that sovereignty itself could be held in trust by the League, which would in turn entrust it to the mandatory power. The implicit assumption here was that sovereignty was more than de facto control: it was, rather, an inherent attribute possessed by any people deserving of the right of self-determination. Only their circumstances of past oppression had made it impossible for the people to exercise the natural sovereignty that they ought to enjoy. The community of civilized nations, acting through its mandates, must exercise sovereignty for them until it could be given to them, the rightful owners.

When the CPA spoke of transferring sovereignty, it seems to have had in mind some incompletely theorized combination of these earlier conceptions. The CPA considered itself to exercise sovereignty in that all civilian matters in Iraq, including the laws, came under the authority of Ambassador Bremer, while military matters fell under the authority of the highest-ranking general in the theater. Bremer could refuse to sign the Governing Council decision recommending the abolition of the Personal Status Code because he was exercising sovereignty and therefore was entitled to decide what Iraqi laws would be changed. All binding decrees issued by the CPA were signed by Bremer, including the November 15 agreement regarding the transfer of sovereignty and a special statute creating the tribunal to try Ba'thist criminals, including Saddam Hussein. Once sovereignty was transferred, however, the CPA no longer had the final say on the laws of Iraq. That responsibility was transferred to the sovereign government, which was to exercise its sovereignty not pursuant to the law of occupation but, in principle, pursuant to the inherent authority of a legitimate government.

The fact that the CPA believed itself to have something called "sovereignty" that it was capable of transferring seems, roughly speaking, to correspond to the Hague conception of sovereignty as something that the occupier exercises in lieu of the rightful government. Yet unlike the Hague model, in which sovereignty is restored to the prewar ruler, sovereignty in Iraq was meant to be transferred to a new, legitimately constituted (if unelected) Iraqi government. The sovereignty that the new government would exercise seemed to be closer to the self-determination sovereignty characteristic of the Covenant of the League of Nations.

Haunting the CPA's usage of the concept of sovereignty was the underlying reality that de facto control over the country sat with the U.S. military, as it continued to do after "sovereignty" was transferred to a new Iraqi transitional government, and as it will even after elections. To be sure, a similar ambiguity existed within the formula whereby the CPA itself came into being. I can vividly recall sitting with the lawyers who had been advising the Office of Reconstruction and Humanitarian Assistance and trying to figure out exactly the legal chain of authority from the president of the United

States, the executive of the chief occupying country, to Ambassador Bremer. Formally speaking, it ran through the secretary of defense; but how, exactly, did it involve the chairman of the Joint Chiefs of Staff, who by statute could take orders from no civilian other than the secretary of defense? The best answer we could find was that the president had divided the powers of occupation into civilian and military components, placing the CPA in charge of the civilian side while leaving the military in charge of security. But of course in practice the military performed any number of "civilian" tasks in Iraq without coming under Ambassador Bremer's command; and despite representing civilian authority, Ambassador Bremer had no capacity, technically speaking, to enforce his commands or Iraqi law, unless it was through the anemic Iraqi police force.

The point is that a "sovereign" Iraqi government cannot realistically have any greater on-the-ground power than did the CPA so long as it lacks the ability to enforce its dictates itself. Technically speaking, Coalition forces remain by request of the Iraqi government, which could at its pleasure revoke its consent and require the Coalition to leave. But the Coalition would no more authorize the new Iraqi government to issue commands to its forces in Iraq than it would have conferred such authority on Ambassador Bremer. U.S. statutory law prohibited Bremer from commanding any troops, and the far stronger force of political reality would bar the way to placing American or other Coalition troops under Iraqi command.

The matter would be no different if an international security force were to take responsibility for providing security in Iraq. Such a force could be led by a UN-authorized command structure, like the one that operated in East Timor, or by a NATO structure like KFOR in Kosovo. If the Iraqi government were considered sovereign by the international community, those forces would be able to remain only if the Iraqi government had agreed to their presence.

No matter what, then, the new Iraqi transitional government was not able at first to exercise the actual control that was once thought to be the sine qua non of sovereignty. It was sovereign in name but not fully in practice. What are we to make of that fact? What are the ethical implications of such an arrangement?

To begin with, let me clarify that the Iraqi government's initial lack of actual control did not mean that the Coalition, whose forces remained in the best position to monopolize the use of violence, was still sovereign. In fact, we were in the presence of a complex, shared model of sovereignty, in which power was to be negotiated between the government and the military forces, no longer properly called by the name "occupiers." As I suggested earlier, even under the CPA, power relations between the occupier and the Governing Council—as well as other important Iraqi political players—were not unidirectional but involved give-and-take. This was even more true, and even more complex, in the posttransfer transitional period. Nominally, the Iraqi government was in charge. But it had to develop a mechanism for communicating with military authorities, or rather scores or hundreds of mechanisms for communicating with commanders at all levels. The more developed the Iraqi political institutions, and the more advanced the Iraqi security services, the fewer the interactions will need to be. But so long as Coalition forces are charged with maintaining order in various sectors of the country, the contact points between the Iraqi government and the Coalition will remain very numerous. And each point of contact represents a potential locus of tension and disagreement.

I raise the issue of the interaction between the Iraqi government and Coalition forces not so much to emphasize the great delicacy of the posttransfer period as to suggest that, during this period, nation building will not have ended. Contrary to popular perception before the fact, in both the United States and Iraq, the formal transfer of sovereignty is not the end of the road. Iraq will not be fully exercising its national capacities until the state has built up a domestic security force capable of enforcing the law. In the descriptive sense, then, Iraq will not enjoy complete sovereignty until its government can actually govern. I do not insist the country must have a military capable of defending its borders from external threat in order to exercise sovereignty in the fullest sense. Plenty of nations, from post–World War II Germany to South Korea today, depend on the presence of foreign forces to help guarantee the national defense, and yet these countries are nonetheless sovereign. But I do wish to argue that until the government can consistently back its legal commands with force, it exercises sovereignty only in a very limited way.[38]

The fact that it will take time for a nominally sovereign Iraqi government to build the actual control requisite for complete sovereignty tells us something important about the former occupier's position relative to the new state. On the one hand, the ethical obligations associated with nation building—including, but not limited to, the responsibility of trusteeship in the exercise of power—will not cease so long as the former occupier's troops remain. Nation building is not over so long as the former occupier continues to be a potentially determinative force in the affairs of the state under construction. The trustee's obligation to subordinate its own interests to those of the nation being built is not lifted just because formal sovereignty has passed.

In practice, that means military commanders who are making judgments about everything from the allocation of supplementary resources to the enforcement of law and order must maintain the ethical stance of trusteeship even though the civilian occupation authorities are gone. This asks a lot of the soldiers, who are trained to put the safety of their own troops above all other objectives, and who will certainly retain this guiding principle, as the American public would want them to do. In my view, the military had the same obligation prior to withdrawal of the civilian occupation—an obligation spectacularly violated in the Abu Ghraib prison—but it would be fair to say that the primary duty to fulfill the obligation fell on the civilians, who in theory, at least, were dictating nation-building priorities. It is entirely possible that leaving the military behind increases the likelihood of conflict between the nation builder's interests and those of the nation being built. But this is the inevitable consequence of withdrawing civilian authority before domestic security structures are in place—and ethically speaking, we have no alternative but to confront it.

On the other hand, it is equally true as an ethical matter that the Coalition as nation builder is under a duty to remain until Iraqi security forces have reached the point where they in fact are capable of maintaining order and enforcing the dictates of a legitimate civilian government. The Coalition must certainly remain engaged through its security forces so long as a transitional government is all that is in place. Troops from other countries could, in theory, substitute, although it seems unlikely as of this writing that many such forces would be forthcoming. But I want to argue for more than that. I want to contend that the nation builder's duties persist until there has arisen a democratically legitimate state that can police its own citizens effectively.

The temptation to withdraw Coalition troops before that has happened will be very great. Liberals who never approved of the war in the first place will be calling for a rapid withdrawal, while conservatives who doubt the efficacy of nation building will also want the troops to come home, since they will perceive that remaining produces diminishing returns. For politicians to admit we must remain in Iraq until there is a stable democracy there might not be a winning campaign strategy. Meanwhile, some significant number of Iraqis will want to see foreign troops out of their country, and they may have a tendency to underestimate the importance of foreign troops as security guarantors. If an elected, legitimate government orders us out, then we must go, even if we think it unwise; but Iraqi public opinion polls alone must not be used as an excuse for an otherwise self-interested decision to depart.

In short, the temptation to withdraw too soon must be resisted. As a practical matter, the goal of nation building—which, as I suggested in the first chapter, is the creation of a stable, basically legitimate democratic state in Iraq—would be ill-served by our beating too hasty a retreat. Producing democracy in Iraq will require constructing an environment in which various parties can all realize that they stand to gain more by cooperation than by defection. Only an external guarantee of security can enable the disparate interest groups in Iraq to overcome coordination costs and reach an agreement. If no agreement is reached, we can expect at best a weak state, and at worst a failed one. The result would be a breeding ground for terror that would make Taliban Afghanistan look benign.

From an ethical standpoint, the duty to remain until an Iraqi government can actually monopolize force is equally strong. Iraqis did not seek foreign intervention that would destroy their state, eliminate their military, and place them in a position where only delicate negotiations and externally imposed security could reestablish basic order. Having thrust the Iraqis into this situation, we have an obligation to enable them to climb out of it. Only nation building fully accomplished is consistent with what will make Iraqi lives better. Abortive nation building, whether abandoned cynically or naïvely, promises Iraqis disaster, not net improvement. That the British abandoned their nation-building project in Iraq knowing full well that it was not completed had much to do with the subsequent miseries suffered by Iraqis—and that is an ethical burden too heavy for any nation builder to bear. Even if we wanted to leave soon after sovereignty were transferred, then, we would not be ethically free to do so. The costs of premature withdrawal are just too great.

Conclusion

BUT IF WE MUST REMAIN AS NATION BUILDERS IN IRAQ beyond the nominal transfer of sovereignty and until an Iraqi government can actually rule its own citizens and enforce its laws, when can we go? At what point are our obligations to Iraq fulfilled, so that responsibility for the Iraqis' fate rests in their own hands? It could possibly be argued that the nation builder's obligation is ongoing, coterminous with the consequences of the nation-building project. If this were the case, then even if Coalition forces left when asked to do so by a legitimate Iraqi government, they could be called back should the government find itself in trouble as a direct result of the weakness of institutions that first came into being when nation building was afoot.[1]

I do not think that the nation builder's obligation to the nation being built remains in full force so long as the consequences of the nation-building exercise remain in play. Our historical sense tells us that the fallout of contingent decisions can linger indefinitely, for decades or even centuries. At some point, the nation builder's special obligations to the country where it has initially participated begin to fade and to look very similar to the obligations of other bystanders who might be called upon to assist. Something special happens when the new nation is able to stand on its own feet, govern itself democratically, and monopolize the means of force in the society. Elections, I have argued, do not constitute magic moments for the transfer of ethical responsibility; but the combined accomplishment of nominal as well as actual sovereignty by a nation that has been under construction does have some ethically meaningful effects.

Mind you, formalism will get us nowhere in serious ethical exploration. The nation builder's obligation will not lift just because, for one discrete moment in time, a new, legitimate government in a country like Iraq has the temporary capacity to monopolize force. If the institutions underlying the state are very weak, or the security forces poised to overthrow the government, or violent secession just waiting in the wings, then the nation builder's duties will not have ended. Under those circumstances, if the new government asks the security forces to remain, then the nation builder really must stay directly involved.

Remaining under some sort of status-of-forces agreement is an ethically subtle business. It will not do for the nation builder to side with whatever government comes to pass. If a new, illegitimate government takes power in a coup, it may be tempting to support it for purposes of stability and security—but then we will have found ourselves back in the quandary of Cold War nation building, which, I have argued, is today both ethically inappropriate and imprudent.

Ultimately, however, because the nation builder is not a parent, and the nation that has been built not a child, the bond of ethical obligation does break when full sovereignty has been achieved. Nations must, at some stage, take responsibility for themselves. "A republic, if you can keep it," is what Franklin reportedly said when asked in Philadelphia what the Constitutional Convention had yielded the American people. The nation builder no more "gives" nationhood than our own Founders "gave" us a republic; but the challenge of keeping it is one that cannot be deferred or delegated. So the nation builder should make a clean break of it, thereby signaling to all sides that nation building has been at least a preliminary success. What we ultimately owe Iraq is to let the Iraqis grasp nationhood and sovereignty for themselves—and to keep it, if they can.

Acknowledgments

EVEN WRITING A SHORT BOOK, ONE ACCRUES DEBTS. Numerous conversations with my New York University School of Law colleague Stephen Holmes stimulated my approach to the questions I discuss here, although I'm still a long way from approaching his ability to juxtapose theoretical abstraction with concrete detail. He, David Golove, Larry Kramer, Richard Pildes, Clay Gillette, and Simon Feldman gave me valuable comments on the manuscript. Heather Schroder and Fred Appel encouraged me to write about my Iraq experiences through the lens of ethical theory, and the Princeton Public Lectures committee graciously invited me to deliver the Walter E. Edge Lectures, in which I was able to develop the argument advanced here in front of an audience that challenged my thinking and, I hope, sharpened it. Heidi Lubov as usual managed everything with characteristic excellence. I also benefited from opportunities to discuss aspects of the argument in seminars hosted at the Carr Center for Human Rights at Harvard University and at the Columbia Law School. I had excellent research assistance from Jesse Wegman at NYU and from Mark Goldberg at the New America Foundation, where I am a fellow. Finally, Jeannie Suk's ideas, especially those about paradox and postcoloniality, have so influenced me that without her I cannot imagine having written this book; but then, through my great good fortune, that is true of everything I do.

Notes

INTRODUCTION

1. Yitzhak Nakash, *The Shi'is of Iraq* (Princeton: Princeton University Press, 1995).

2. See, e.g., Kanan Makiya, *Republic of Fear: The Politics of Modern Iraq* (Berkeley and Los Angeles: University of California Press, 1998), 142, 178.

3. The claim of authorization depended on UN Security Council Resolution 1441 (2002), which recalled a prior warning of "serious consequences" for continued Iraqi violations of weapons-disclosure obligations, and found Iraq to be "in material breach" of those obligations. Neither UN Security Council Resolution 1511 (2003) nor UN Security Council Resolution 1546 (2004) expressly recognized the legality of the war or what both called the "occupation."

4. Beyond the canonical Michael Walzer, *Just and Unjust Wars* (New York: Basic Books, 1992), see recently and prominently: *Humanitarian Intervention: Ethical, Legal, and Political Dilemmas*, ed. J. L. Holzgrefe and Robert Keohane (New York: Cambridge University Press, 2003); *Ethics and Foreign Intervention*, ed. Deen K. Chatterjee and Don E. Scheid (Cambridge: Cambridge University Press, 2003); David Rieff, *A Bed for the Night: Humanitarianism in Crisis* (New York: Simon & Schuster, 2002); and Stanley Hoffmann, with Robert C. Johansen, James P. Sterba, and Raimo Väyrynen, *The Ethics and Politics of Humanitarian Intervention* (Notre Dame: Notre Dame University Press, 1996).

5. An early leader is Michael Ignatieff, *Empire Lite: Nation-Building in Bosnia, Kosovo and Afghanistan* (London: Vintage, 2003). Another excellent early entry is Simon Chesterman, *You, the People: The United Nations, Transitional Administration, and State-Building* (Oxford: Oxford University Press, 2004). See also articles by Walzer on failed states and on the Iraq war originally published in *Dissent* and now reproduced in Michael Walzer, *Arguing about War* (New Haven: Yale University Press, 2004).

6. Richard Holbrooke, *To End a War* (New York: Knopf, 1999); Wesley Clark, *Waging Modern War: Bosnia, Kosovo, and the Future of Combat* (New York: Public Affairs, 2001).

7. Ruti Teitel, *Transitional Justice* (Oxford: Oxford University Press, 2002); Gary Jonathan Bass, *Stay the Hand of Vengeance: The Politics of War Crimes Tribunals* (Princeton: Princeton University Press, 2000).

8. See James Dobbins et al., *America's Role in Nation-Building: From Germany to Iraq* (Santa Monica, Calif.: RAND, 2003), and bibliography there. Particularly valuable are a series of International Crisis Group reports on Bosnia and Kosovo. See also Adam Przeworski, ed., *Sustainable Democracy* (Cambridge: Cambridge University Press, 1995); Timothy D. Sisk, *Power Sharing and International Mediation in Ethnic Conflicts* (Washington, D.C.: United States Institute of Peace / Carnegie Commission on Preventing Deadly Conflict, 1996); Krishna Kumar, ed., *Postconflict Elections, Democratization, and International Assistance* (Boulder, Colo.: Lynne Rienner, 1998); Benjamin Reilly, *Democracy in Divided Societies: Electoral Engineering for Conflict Management* (Cambridge: Cambridge University Press, 2001).

9. Authors proposing such an approach include Peter Lyon, "The Rise and Fall and Possible Revival of International Trusteeship," *Journal of Commonwealth and Comparative Politics* 31, no. 1 (1993): 96; Richard Caplan, *A New Trusteeship? The International Administration of War-Torn Territories*, Adelphi Paper 341 (New York: Oxford University Press for IISS, 2002); Tom Parker, *The Ultimate Intervention: Revitalising the UN Trusteeship Council for the Twenty-first Century* (Sandvika: Norwegian School of Management, 2003). On the other side of the debate, prominent voices include Robert Jackson, *The Global Covenant: Human Conduct in a World of States* (New York: Oxford University Press, 2000); Jackson's student William Bain, *Between Anarchy and Society: Trusteeship and the Obligations of Power* (New York: Oxford University Press, 2003); Ruth E. Gordon, "Legal Problems with Trusteeship," *Cornell International Law Journal* 28 (1995): 301. The Afghanistan and Iraq wars generated a flurry of short articles proposing and criticizing international trusteeship options in these contexts.

10. Compare the use of first-person narrative to explore ethical problems in David Kennedy, *The Dark Sides of Virtue: Reassessing International Humanitarianism* (Princeton: Princeton University Press, 2004), 35–107, 284–96.

11. I have in mind not so much the Althusserian interpellative "Hey, you!" as the (ethical?) implicative "Hey, we!"

CHAPTER ONE
NATION BUILDING: OBJECTIVES

1. This is inevitably a cursory characterization of a complex subject; the creation of markets for American goods was naturally at work alongside containment. But at all events capitalism and the creation of allies were more important than creating internal political legitimacy. On the reasons for the Marshall Plan, and George Kennan's views in particular, see Diane B. Kunz, "The Marshall Plan Re-

considered: A Complex of Motives," *Foreign Affairs* 76, no. 3 (1997): 162; and more generally the Marshall Plan Commemorative Section in that issue of *Foreign Affairs*. See also Michael J. Hogan, *The Marshall Plan: America, Britain, and the Reconstruction of Western Europe* (Cambridge: Cambridge University Press, 1987). On Japan, see, e.g., John Dower, *Embracing Defeat: Japan in the Wake of World War II* (New York: W. W. Norton, 1999); Michael Schaller, *The American Occupation of Japan* (Oxford: Oxford University Press, 1985).

2. See classically Amos Tversky and Daniel Kahneman, "Availability: A Heuristic for Judging Frequency and Probability," *Cognitive Psychology* 5 (1973): 207–32; and more generally Amos Tversky and Daniel Kahneman, eds., *Judgment under Uncertainty* (New York: Cambridge University Press, 1982).

3. Countries like Iran and Syria support terror against Israel in large part because Israel cannot fully deter them. But even they do so by way of Lebanon, a weak state, in order to have some deniability.

4. See, e.g., Gilles Kepel, *Jihad: The Trail of Political Islam* (Cambridge: Harvard University Press, 2001).

5. There are thus essentially three ideal types of states that generate terror: those that export terror by supporting it financially abroad; those that are too weak to suppress terror or terror training within; and those that unintentionally generate terror against themselves and others by means of their own illegitimacy. I am grateful to Stephen Holmes for helping me sharpen this distinction. For some very preliminary empirical support for the connection between illegitimacy and terrorism, based on very limited data, see Alan B. Krueger and Jitka Malecková, "Seeking the Roots of Terrorism," *Chronicle of Higher Education* 49, no. 39 (June 6, 2003), B10 ("Apart from population—larger countries tend to have more terrorists—the only variable that was consistently associated with the number of terrorists was the Freedom House index of political rights and civil liberties. Countries with more freedom were less likely to be the birthplace of international terrorists. Poverty and literacy were unrelated to the number of terrorists from a country. Think of a country like Saudi Arabia: It is wealthy but has few political and civil freedoms. Perhaps it is no coincidence that so many of the September 11 terrorists—and Osama bin Laden himself—came from there"); Alan B. Krueger and Jitka Malecková, "Education, Poverty, and Terrorism: Is There a Causal Connection?" *Journal of Economic Perspectives* 17, no. 4 (2003): 119–44; National Bureau of Economic Research Working Paper No. W9074 (July 2002). The central argument of these articles is that poverty and lack of education are not the best predictors of terrorism. For further empirical analysis of terrorist strategy, also based on small data sets, see Robert A. Pape, "The Strategic Logic of Suicide Terrorism," *American Political Science Review* 97 (2003): 343–61.

6. See Kepel, *Jihad*.

7. I pursue this argument at much greater length in *After Jihad: America and the Struggle for Islamic Democracy* (New York: Farrar, Straus and Giroux, 2003).

8. See Ignatieff, *Empire Lite.*

9. Max Weber, "Politik als Beruf," in *Gesammelte politische Schriften* (Munich: Drei Masken Verlag, 1921), 396–450.

10. A related objection would accept the permissibility of engaging others as means but would object that in so doing we are privileging our own interests over theirs. I owe the distinction to Simon Feldman.

11. Cf. Kant, *The Metaphysical Principles of Virtue*, trans. James Ellington (Indianapolis: Bobbs Merrill, 1964), 117: "Benevolence is the satisfaction one takes in the happiness (well-being) of others. But beneficence is the maxim to make the happiness of others an end for oneself, and the duty of beneficence involves the subject's being constrained by his reason to adopt this maxim as a universal law. . . . It is a duty of every man to be beneficent, i.e., to be helpful to men in need according to one's means, for the sake of their happiness and without hoping for anything thereby. For every man who finds himself in need wishes that he might be helped by other men. But if he should make known his maxim of not wanting to give assistance in turn to others in their need—if he should make such a maxim a universal permissive law—then everyone would likewise refuse him assistance when he was in need, or at least everyone would be entitled to refuse. Thus the selfish maxim conflicts with itself when it is made a universal law, i.e., it is contrary to duty. Consequently, the altruistic maxim of beneficence toward those in need is a universal duty of men; this is so because they are to be regarded as fellow men, i.e., as needy rational beings, united by nature in one dwelling place for mutual aid."

12. See Kenneth J. Arrow, *Social Choice and Individual Values* (New Haven: Yale University Press, 1970). For an account of the relation between Condorcet and Arrow, see Richard H. Pildes and Elizabeth S. Anderson, "Slinging Arrows at Democracy: Social Choice Theory, Value Pluralism, and Democratic Politics," *Columbia Law Review* 90 (1990): 2121, 2129–35.

13. These issues are well explored in a series of articles in the December 2002 issue of the journal *Legal Theory* (vol. 8, no. 4). In that issue, see Scott J. Shapiro, "Law, Plans, and Practical Reason," 387; Philip Pettit, "Collective Persons and Powers," 443; Christopher Kutz, "The Collective Work of Citizenship," 471; John Gardner, "Reasons for Teamwork," 495; Michael E. Bratman, "Shapiro on Legal Positivism and Jointly Intentional Activity," 511.

14. I do not wish to enter here the debate over whether only democracy can serve a people's interests; other decent forms of government may exist, as well. Cf. John Rawls, *The Law of Peoples* (Cambridge: Harvard University Press, 1999); *Political Liberalism* (New York: Columbia University Press, 1993). But if the overwhelming majority of citizens consider the government legitimate and if all citizens' rights are respected, it is difficult to see how this outcome could be against the citizens' interests.

15. Of course the way that Germany and Japan fell under U.S. domination affects the morality of these nation-building efforts; we certainly have less moral

claim to making Iraqis an offer they cannot refuse. But I mean the example only to emphasize that instrumental motives are no bar to moral permissibility.

16. See David Golove and Allen Buchanan, "Philosophy of International Law," in *Oxford Handbook of Jurisprudence and Philosophy of Law,* ed. Jules L. Coleman, Kenneth Himma, and Scott J. Shapiro (New York: Oxford University Press, 2002), 838–934.

17. Cf. Thomas Pogge, *Realizing Rawls* (Ithaca: Cornell University Press, 1989); see also Buchanan and Golove, "Philosophy of International Law," 904.

18. See Weber, "Politik als Beruf."

19. On the intervening decade, see Dobbins et al., *America's Role in Nation-Building,* 78–83; see also David Bentley, "Operation Uphold Democracy: Military Support for Democracy in Haiti," *Strategic Forum,* no. 78 (June 1996).

20. On present conditions, including the restoration of the heroin trade, see Barnett Rubin et al., "Building a New Afghanistan: The Value of Success, the Cost of Failure" (Center on International Cooperation Policy Paper, March 2004). On pre-Taliban Afghanistan, see Barnett Rubin, *The Fragmentation of Afghanistan* (New Haven: Yale University Press, 1995).

21. Henry A. Foster, *The Making of Modern Iraq: A Product of World Forces* (New York: Russell and Russell, 1935).

22. Matthew Eliot, *"Independent Iraq": The Monarchy and British Influence 1941–1958* (London: Tauris, 1996).

23. David Fromkin, *A Peace to End All Peace: The Fall of the Ottoman Empire and the Creation of the Modern Middle East* (New York: Owl Books, 2001).

24. Toby Dodge, *Inventing Iraq: The Failure of Nation Building and a History Denied* (New York: Columbia University Press, 2003).

25. In a fascinating essay, "The Laws of War in Occupied Territory," read to the Grotius Society in February 1932, Sir Arnold Wilson, the onetime civil commissioner of Iraq (that is, the L. Paul Bremer of his day) outlined some advice for nation builders based on his Mesopotamian experience. One key point was that it was "essential" for the administrators to "know the local language." *Transactions of the Grotius Society* 18 (1933): 20.

26. For a couple of months in 2003, most of the beds were moved out of the building as the CPA staff took up residence in the Al Rashid Hotel. This arrangement didn't last, though. After a series of mortar attacks on the hotel, the American civilians retreated to the relative safety of the palace, deeper inside the green zone, and therefore farther from mortar fire or the occasional truck bomb. The spot I once occupied on the kitchen floor has not yet been vacated as of this writing.

27. Hamilton's disclaimers of dominant presidential power in *The Federalist Papers* come to mind. See, e.g., John Lamberton Harper, *American Machiavelli: Alexander Hamilton and the Origins of U.S. Foreign Policy* (Cambridge: Cambridge University Press, 2004).

28. The importance of the *hawza* of Qom is far more recent, dating only to the 1920s and the arrival of ʿAbd al-Karim Haʾeri of Yazd. See Roy Mottahedeh, *The Mantle of the Prophet: Religion and Politics in Iran* (Oxford: One World, 2000), 228–29.

29. It is sometimes said that Bakr al-Hakim was affiliated with the reformist wing of the Iranian clerical hierarchy and with President Mohammed Khatami. However, Bakr al-Hakim was skilled enough as a politician to broaden his support beyond this reformist base.

30. Thus even al-Qaʿida, which considers Shiʿi Muslims to be unbelievers, disclaimed responsibility for the March 2004 bombings of Shiʿi shrines in Kadhimiyya and Karbala on the holiday of ʿAshura. Al-Qaʿida is always attuned to its Arab and Muslim audiences, who are reluctant to tolerate attacks on praying Muslims of whatever denomination.

31. Muqtada occasionally sought to deepen his institutional position by claiming the support of Ayatollah Kazem Husayn Haʾeri, resident during the occupation and for the years before it in Qom. Haʾeri had studied with Muqtada's late father, and himself had pretensions to clerical authority in Iraq; his relationship to Muqtada was therefore complex.

32. The English text reads, in Sistani's approved translation:

> In the Name of The Almighty
> Those forces have no jurisdiction whatsoever to appoint members of the Constitution preparation assembly. Also there is no guarantee either that this assembly will prepare a constitution that serves the best interests of the Iraqi people or express their national identity whose backbone is sound Islamic religion and noble social values. The said plan is unacceptable from the outset. First of all there must be a general election so that every Iraqi citizen—who is eligible to vote—can choose someone to represent him in a foundational Constitution preparation assembly. Then the drafted Constitution can be put to a referendum. All believers must insist on the accomplishment of this crucial matter and contribute to achieving it in the best way possible.
> May Allah The Blessed Almighty, guide everyone to that which is good and beneficial.
> Wassalamu alaikum warahmatullah wabarakatuh
> (Peace and Allah's love and blessings be upon you)
> Signed & Sealed
> Ali Al-Hussaini Al-Seestani
> 25 Rabiul-Akhar 1424
> 26 June 2003

33. United Nations Security Council Resolution 1546 calls for elections no later than January 31, 2005.

34. Cf. Adam Przeworski, *Democracy and the Market* (Cambridge: Cambridge University Press, 1991), 30–34.

35. Cf. John C. Calhoun, *A Disquisition on Government* (Columbia, S.C.: S. Johnston, 1851): "[I]t is manifest, that this [constitutional] provision must be of a character calculated to prevent any one interest, or combination of interests, from using the powers of government to aggrandize itself at the expense of the others. Here lies the evil: and just in proportion as it shall prevent, or fail to prevent it, in the same degree it will effect, or fail to effect the end intended to be accomplished. There is but one certain mode in which this result can be secured; and that is, by the adoption of some restriction or limitation, which shall so effectually prevent any one interest, or combination of interests, from obtaining the exclusive control of the government, as to render hopeless all attempts directed to that end. There is, again, but one mode in which this can be effected; and that is, by taking the sense of each interest or portion of the community, which may be unequally and injuriously affected by the action of the government, separately, through its own majority, or in some other way by which its voice may be fairly expressed; and to require the consent of each interest, either to put or to keep the government in action."

36. As Dodge shows, in fact the British strategy changed several times; by the last stage the goal was to declare victory and get out as soon as possible, damn the consequences. It need hardly be added that this is a recipe for failure we cannot afford to repeat.

CHAPTER TWO

TRUSTEESHIP, PATERNALISM, AND SELF-INTEREST

1. On the proper translation, see Eyal Benvenisti, *The International Law of Occupation* (Princeton: Princeton University Press, 1993), 7 n. 1. "Public order and civil life" is preferred, although "public order and safety" is often used.

2. Except to the extent modified by Geneva Convention obligations or the occupier's decrees. See ibid., chap. 2.

3. Francisco de Vitoria, *De indis et de iure belli relectiones* (1696), trans. John Pawley Bate (Washington, D.C.: Carnegie Institution, 1917).

4. "They must grant to me in my turn, that all political power which is set over men, and that all privilege claimed or exercised in exclusion of them, being wholly artificial, and for so much, a derogation from the natural equality of mankind at large, ought to be some way or other exercised ultimately for their benefit. If this is true with regard to every species of political dominion, and every descrip-

tion of commercial privilege, none of which can be original self-derived rights, or grants for the mere private benefit of the holders, then such rights, or privileges, or whatever else you choose to call them, are all in the strictest sense a trust; and it is of the very essence of every trust to be rendered accountable; and even totally to cease, when it substantially varies from the purposes for which alone it could have a lawful existence." Edmund Burke, Speech on Fox's East India Bill, December 1, 1783, in *The Writing and Speeches of Edmund Burke*, vol. 5, *India: Madras and Bengal*, ed. P. J. Marshall (Oxford: Clarendon Press,1981), 385. Cf. Ramendra Nath Chowdhuri, *International Mandates and Trusteeship Systems: A Comparative Study* (The Hague: M. Nijhoff, 1955), 19; Lyon,"The Rise and Fall and Possible Revival of International Trusteeship," 97 n. 6.

5. See Benvenisti, *The International Law of Occupation*.

6. Hague IV: Convention Respecting the Laws and Customs of War on Land (1907), Arts. 43, 46–48, 55.

7. Article 22 of the Covenant of the League of Nations.

8. Ibid.

9. Ibid.

10. See Chesterman, *You, the People*.

11. United Nations Security Council Resolution 1483 (2003): "5. Calls upon all concerned to comply fully with their obligations under international law including in particular the Geneva Conventions of 1949 and the Hague Regulations of 1907."

12. See Benvenisti, *The International Law of Occupation*, preface to the new edition (2004), and cf. his argument in the older edition that occupation law is moribund.

13. Economists and lawyers use the word "agency" differently. For the former, an agent is anyone who performs some action on behalf of another pursuant to some agreement; the "costs of agency" are relevant, therefore, to a wide range of relationships, including trusteeship. By contrast, lawyers tend to speak of fiduciary relationships as those in which one person acts on behalf of another and is subject to certain duties of varying types. For them, an agent is a particular kind of person acting on behalf of another, owing a particular type of duty; and trusteeship is not an agency relationship. I use the term "agent" in its economic sense here. See classically Michael C. Jensen and William H. Meckling, "Theory of the Firm: Managerial Behaviour, Agency Costs and Ownership Structure," *Journal of Financial Economics* 3 (1976): 305.

14. Burke, Speech on Fox's East India Bill.

15. Speech at the Conclusion of the Poll on November 3, 1774, in *The Writing and Speeches of Edmund Burke*, vol. 3, *Party, Parliament, and the American War 1774–1780*, ed. Warren M. Elofson, with John A. Woods (Oxford: Clarendon Press, 1996), 69.

16. See, e.g., Jonathan R. Macey, "Promoting Public-Regarding Legislation through Statutory Interpretation: An Interest Group Model," *Columbia Law Review*

86 (1986): 223, 244–45: "The formation of a representative democracy, where voters elect legislators to run the enterprise of government, establishes what economists refer to as an 'agency relationship.' An agency relationship calls for one person or group of people (the principal) to hire another person or group of people (the agent) to perform services and make decisions on the principal's behalf. . . . Elected officials, like all agents, are rational economic actors; they are inevitably more concerned with maximizing their own utility than with maximizing the utility of their principals. This divergence of interests (called 'agency costs') is an unwanted but inevitable feature inherent in any principal-agent relationship—including, perhaps especially, the one that exists between voters and their elected representatives."

17. This assumes effective regulation of corruption and is part of the reason we consider bribe taking or other corrupt behavior by elected officials to be unethical. See Susan Rose-Ackerman, *Corruption and Government: Causes, Consequences, and Reform* (Cambridge: Cambridge University Press, 1999).

18. Of course Burke is often invoked for the latter position, on the strength of his comments to the Bristol electors.

19. Cf. Benvenisti's argument that conflicts of interest arise between occupier and occupied, *The International Law of Occupation*, 210, 213–14.

20. Dodge, *Inventing Iraq*, 31–41.

21. See, e.g., Walter L. Nossaman and Joseph L. Wyatt, Jr., *Trust Administration and Taxation* (New York: Matthew Bender & Company, 2004) § 34.12 [1].

22. Cf. Wilson, "The Laws of War in Occupied Territory," 24.

23. There is a niche how-to literature designed for such advising. See, e.g., Przeworski, *Sustainable Democracy*; Sisk, *Power Sharing and International Mediation in Ethnic Conflicts*; Kumar, *Postconflict Elections, Democratization, and International Assistance*; and Reilly, *Democracy in Divided Societies*. But successful institutions cannot be built on the basis of a menu of options in which the nation builder chooses a president or parliamentary system from column A, judicial review from column B, and a type of federalism from column C. There is a strong empirical literature on electoral systems and outcomes—but hybridization and political compromise mean that advice given on that basis may misfire. For the example of Fiji, see Chesterman, *You, the People*, 213–14.

24. See, e.g., Misha Glenny, *The Fall of Yugoslavia: The Third Balkan War* (New York: Penguin Books, 1996); Mark Thompson, *A Paper House: The Ending of Yugoslavia* (New York: Pantheon Books, 1992).

25. Cf. Przeworski, *Sustainable Democracy*, 5.

26. The literature on civil society is voluminous, but for one influential approach, see Jürgen Habermas, *The Structural Transformation of the Public Sphere: An Inquiry into a Category of Bourgeois Society* (Cambridge: MIT Press, 1991); Craig Calhoun, ed., *Habermas and the Public Sphere* (Cambridge: MIT Press, 1992).

27. Przeworski, *Sustainable Democracy*, 5–6.

28. See, e.g., Robert Kaplan, *Balkan Ghosts: A Journey through History* (New York: St. Martin's, 1993); *The Coming Anarchy: Shattering the Dreams of the Post Cold War* (New York: Random House, 2000).

29. Robert Nozick, *Anarchy, State, and Utopia* (New York: Basic Books, 1974), 12–25.

30. Of course many such associations are meant not only to serve the good of mutual protection, but also to enhance individual gain. For a game-theoretic account of how nationalist or ethnic identification may be driven by such self-serving interest, see Russell Hardin, *One for All: The Logic of Group Conflict* (Princeton: Princeton University Press, 1995), 49–60. Hardin's emphasis is on conflict over distributional goods.

31. But not, of course, no need at all. My argument is for the effects of anarchy in generating ethnic and denominational loyalties.

32. See Dobbins et al., *America's Role in Nation-Building*; see also William J. Darch, "Introduction to Anarchy: Humanitarian Intervention and State-Building in Somalia," in *UN Peacekeeping, American Policy, and the Uncivil Wars of the 1990s* (New York: St. Martin's Press, 1996), 311.

33. It is conceivable, though unlikely, that things might get so bad in Iraq that our presence could become an active impediment to the emergence of security— and if that were to occur, we would be ethically obligated to withdraw.

34. Cf. Stephen John Stedman, "Spoiler Problems in Peace Processes," *International Security* 22 (1997): 5.

35. The Japanese constitution was notoriously written by Americans in English and translated into Japanese. Ray A. Moore and Donald L. Robinson, *Partners for Democracy—Crafting the New Japanese State under MacArthur* (New York: Oxford University Press, 2004). The German constitution was German-written, but under U.S. supervision. See, e.g., Donald P. Kommers, *The Constitutional Jurisprudence of the Federal Republic of Germany* (Durham: Duke University Press, 1997).

36. See James A. Gardner, *Legal Imperialism: American Lawyers and Foreign Aid in Latin America* (Madison: University of Wisconsin Press, 1980).

37. On the authorship of African constitutions and their discontents, see Julian Go, "Modeling the State: Postcolonial Constitutions in Asia and Africa," *Southeast Asian Studies* 39, no. 4 (2002): 558, 561–64; see also Muna Ndulo, "The Democratization Process and Structural Adjustment in Africa," *Indiana Journal of Global Legal Studies* 10 (2003): 315, 317–18.

38. See E. E. Evans Pritchard, "The Nuer of Southern Sudan," in *African Political Systems*, ed. M. Fortes and E. E. Evans Pritchard (Oxford: Oxford University Press, 1940), 272, 291–95.

39. For examples, see Dennis Ross, *The Missing Peace: The Inside Story of the Fight for Middle East Peace* (New York: Farrar, Straus and Giroux, 2004).

40. TAL, Art. 7. The provisions also ban laws that contradict the principles of democracy, an innovation in the document.

41. John Kerry, "A Strategy for Iraq," *Washington Post*, April 13, 2004, A19.

42. For a complex view, see Ignatieff, *Empire Lite*.

43. See "East Timor, the Building of a Nation: An Interview with Sergio Vieira de Mello," *Europa Magazine*, November 2001.

44. See, e.g., Jarat Chopra, "The UN's Kingdom of East Timor," *Survival* 42, no. 3 (2000): 27–39.

45. For an excellent discussion, see Chesterman, *You, the People*, 126–53.

CHAPTER THREE

THE MAGIC OF ELECTIONS AND THE WAY HOME

1. Qur'an 3:159.

2. Qur'an 42:38.

3. Eventually the CPA insignia was supplemented by the vaguely socialist-sounding GC slogan: "We shall all participate in building the new Iraq!"

4. Of course some nation-building exercises in transitional administrations have featured many elections as part of the process, with notoriously poor results. The literature on elections in nation building is growing. For a good introduction, see Chesterman, *You, the People*, 204–35; see also Caplan, *A New Trusteeship?*, 40–42.

5. "My propositions serve as elucidations in the following way: anyone who understands them eventually recognizes them as nonsensical, when he has used them—as steps—to climb up beyond them. (He must, so to speak, throw away the ladder after he has climbed up it.)" Ludwig Wittgenstein, *Tractatus Logico-Philosophicus*, trans. D. F. Pears and Brian McGuiness (London: Routledge, 2001), 6.54.

6. This fear is salient in the technical debate about whether national or local elections should come first. See, e.g., Juan J. Linz and Alfred C. Stepan, *Problems of Democratic Transition and Consolidation: Southern Europe, South America, and Post-Communist Europe* (Baltimore: Johns Hopkins University Press, 1996), 98–107; Larry Jay Diamond, *Developing Democracy: Toward Consolidation* (Baltimore: Johns Hopkins University Press, 1999), 158; Benjamin Reilly, "Post-Conflict Elections: Constraints and Dangers," *International Peacekeeping* 9, no. 2 (2002): 118, 120.

7. Cf. Richard Holbrooke's concerns, quoted in Caplan, *A New Trusteeship?*, 41, that fascists and separatists might be elected in Bosnia. Caplan argues that the Dayton timetable "allowed too little time for new thinking to emerge that might produce a realignment of political forces."

8. The phrase is originally Edward Djerejian's.

9. On Kosovo, for example, see Chesterman, *You, the People*, 226–30.

10. See ibid., 231–33; but for a dissenting view, see Jarat Chopra, "Building State Failure in East Timor," *Development and Change* 33 (2002): 979.

11. See Chesterman, *You, the People*, 208.

12. Ibid., 226–30.

13. See Feldman, *After Jihad*, and sources cited at 234n.

14. The Schlesingers, father and son, are associated with the claim that swings in the United States occur on average every sixteen or seventeen years. See, e.g., Arthur M. Schlesinger, Jr., *The Cycles of American History* (Boston: Houghton Mifflin, 1986). Other sorts of estimates abound. See, e.g., Joshua Goldstein, *Long Cycles: Prosperity and War in the Modern Age* (New Haven: Yale University Press, 1988).

15. The literature on elections is enormous. For what is still a useful introduction, see generally Robert Dahl, *Polyarchy: Participation and Opposition* (New Haven: Yale University Press, 1971). See also Dennis C. Mueller, *Public Choice III* (Cambridge: Cambridge University Press, 2003).

16. This is not to discount a healthy skepticism about elections as preference-revealing: "[A]ccurate preference-aggregation through politics is unlikely to be accomplished in the light of the conundrums in developing a social welfare function. Public choice theory has shown that cycling problems, strategic and manipulative behavior, sheer chance and other factors make majoritarianism highly unlikely to provide an accurate aggregation of preferences." Cass R. Sunstein, "Constitutions and Democracies: An Epilogue," in *Constitutionalism and Democracy*, ed. Jon Elster and Rune Slagstad (Cambridge: Cambridge University Press, 1988), 327, 335.

17. For a sophisticated and detailed account of the analogy, see Samuel Issacharoff and Richard H. Pildes, "Politics as Markets: Partisan Lockups of the Democratic Process," *Stanford Law Review* 50 (1998): 643.

18. The pervasive use of polling is itself a fascinating feature of contemporary nation building: loosely democratic in aspiration, but also oddly incongruous where nation builders will not stand for election.

19. Elections also push politicians to explain their views to voters—or to try to create demand for their views by advertising, and so forth.

20. Cf. Bruce Ackerman, *We the People*, vol. 1 (Cambridge: Harvard University Press, 1998).

21. Compare Paddy Ashdown's observation, cited by Chesterman, *You, the People*, 207, that after seven years of repeated elections, "the people of Bosnia have grown weary of voting."

22. Consider the first South African elections, in which participation was high although the victory of the ANC was assured.

23. Amy Chua, *World on Fire: How Exporting Free Market Democracy Breeds Ethnic Hatred and Global Instability* (New York: Doubleday, 2003).

24. Fareed Zakaria, *The Future of Freedom: Illiberal Democracy at Home and Abroad* (New York: W. W. Norton, 2003).

25. And, according to one interpretation of Hutu-Tutsi differences, in Rwanda. See Mahmood Mamdani, *When Victims Become Killers: Colonialism, Nativism, and the Genocide in Rwanda* (Princeton: Princeton University Press, 2002). Chua cites the Tutsi as a market-dominant minority, and indeed the question is a complex one.

26. Chua, *World on Fire*, 14.

27. Iraqi Jews—the very model of a market-dominant minority, so prevalent in financial markets that the British insisted that the minister of finance be a Jew—emigrated or were expelled in the years after the 1948 war in which Iraq joined other Arab states in invading Israel. See Elie Kedourie, "The Kingdom of Iraq: A Retrospect," in Elie Kedourie, *The Chatham House Version and Other Middle-Eastern Studies* (Chicago: Ivan R. Dee, 2004), 236.

28. Indeed it is hard to see how redistribution will ever occur if it is not driven by electoral mandate. The self-preserving instincts of market-dominant minorities do not typically extend to such liberality.

29. Zakaria, *The Future of Freedom*, 105–13.

30. *New York Trust Co. v. Eisner*, 256 U.S. 345, 349 (1921).

31. There were, however, modifications from classical law in the codified law. But familiar features of shari'a were retained, including polygamy (with judicial permission) and divorce on classical *talaq* principles. Judicial divorce at the wife's initiative was permitted under some conditions. For a useful summary, see Dawoud El Alami and Doreen Hinchcliffe, *Islamic Marriage and Divorce Laws of the Arab World* (London: Kluwer Law International, 1996).

32. The treatise was *Adwa' 'ala qanun al-ahwal al-shakhsiyya al-'iraqi* (Najaf: Na'man Press, 1963). For a detailed discussion of the treatise, see the excellent article by Chibli Mallat, "Shi'ism and Sunnism in Iraq: Revisiting the Codes," in *Islamic Family Law*, ed. Chibli Mallat and Jane Connors (London: Graham & Trotman, 1990), 81.

33. A complex legal anomaly arises from this circumstance: the TAL, meant to govern after transfer of sovereignty, was said to require CPA approval given before sovereignty was transferred. Once sovereignty passed, however, there was no legal reason the TAL should not be amendable by the interim government, on its own terms. Furthermore, the legal effect of the TAL after June 30, 2004, was uncertain, apparently resting more on the voluntary compliance of the government than on any other basis. UN Security Council Resolution 1546 recognizing the transitional government made no mention of the TAL after Sistani sent a letter to the president of the Council warning that any such reference would have "serious consequences."

34. Senate pressure mattered here, as it did when Bremer stated publicly that he would not sign a TAL that was "too Islamic." The divergence of interests between occupier and occupied was clearly in play.

35. Nasir Kamil Chadirchi, son of Kamil Chadirchi. Today Chadirchi is head of the National Democratic Party, the same party his father headed for decades before the Ba'thists suppressed political dissent.

36. Arguably, the British-built institutions of the constitutional monarchy lasted until 1958. Would we consider our efforts in Iraq a success if the institutions we helped build lasted thirty years?

37. Hague Regulations, Art. 43.

38. There is a large literature on sovereignty, actual and theoretical, the continuum on which it rests, and its different types. To begin, see Keohane's essay "Political Authority after Intervention: Gradations in Sovereignty," in Holzgrefe and Keohane, *Humanitarian Intervention*. See also Abram Chayes and Antonia Handler Chayes, *The New Sovereignty: Compliance with International Regulatory Agreements* (Cambridge: Harvard University Press, 1997); Anne-Marie Slaughter, *A New World Order* (Princeton: Princeton University Press, 2004).

CONCLUSION

1. On the duty of former colonizers, see, e.g., William Pfaff, "A New Colonialism," in *Foreign Affairs* 74, no. 1 (January–February 1995): 2–6.

Index